T0158745

Jim Lozen

Memories from a Past Life

iUniverse, Inc.
Bloomington

Memories from a Past Life

The views expressed in this work are solely those of the author and do not necessarily reflect the views of the publisher, and the publisher hereby disclaims any responsibility for them.
iUniverse books may be ordered through booksellers or by contacting:

iUniverse
1663 Liberty Drive
Bloomington, IN 47403
www.iuniverse.com
1-800-Authors (1-800-288-4677)

Because of the dynamic nature of the Internet, any web addresses or links contained in this book may have changed since publication and may no longer be valid. The views expressed in this work are solely those of the author and do not necessarily reflect the views of the publisher, and the publisher hereby disclaims any responsibility for them.

Any people depicted in stock imagery provided by Thinkstock are models, and such images are being used for illustrative purposes only.

Certain stock imagery © Thinkstock.

ISBN: 978-1-4620-3680-6 (sc)
ISBN: 978-1-4620-3682-0 (e)
ISBN: 978-1-4620-3681-3 (dj)

Library of Congress Control Number: 2011912858

Printed in the United States of America

iUniverse rev. date: 7/27/2011

7-4-96
Fourth of July

The Fourth of July reminds me of Vietnam, with all of the noise and racket going on. I wish I could go deaf just once a year, and then I wouldn't have to hear, because if I close my eyes for just a minute or two I'll go back to Nam and all the bloodshed that I once went through.

I start shivering and shaking, and I've got all of these thoughts running through my mind, thoughts I haven't had for such a long time. If I could go deaf just once a year, it would be on the Fourth of July so I wouldn't hear.

9-20-98
Awakening

We came together, there were four in all, joined in celebration, because we had answered the call. We spread the word the best we could, and before you knew it, other people joined the brotherhood.

We have spread throughout the land, and the spiritual awakening is now at hand. It will take some time, like all things do, but the spiritual awakening will come through you. No need to prod like others do. The awakening will just happen. It will dawn on you.

1-15-01
A Dime a Dozen

Friends are a dime a dozen, but what would you do without these friends that are also part of you? They give you this force, this field of energy that makes us all one, you and me. They don't know this, they don't even understand, but the energy we create, created this land. We create this energy every day, even our deceased brothers, because they didn't just fade away.

They gave to this world the ultimate dream, when they made the choice to become part of the energy scheme. This world is our mother, father, brother, even little sister too, because you can't destroy the energy that's within me and you.

Death is an adventure, another chapter in the book of dreams that will only appear as real as you want it to seem.

1-27-02
A Dreamer's Dream

Sunlight from heaven, God above; energy is all that we are made of. Energy surrounds this planet of mine, energy and love for all time. Life is an illusion, a dream if you will, that starts from the moment of birth and always will.

Negative or positive, it's all in your dream, whatever you will, is as it should seem. Domestication, the dreamer's dead end, it's handed down from generation to generation, and it isn't your Friend. Dreamers dream the world as it should be, and domestication knocks it back into reality.

11-16-03
A Living Hell

There is no Devil, there is no time as well, this right here is our living Hell. The aging process that was created by man was created with negative energy that he just really doesn't understand! Negative energy, positive too, both have certain qualities that we can use.

A man in a rowboat, rowing to shore, or a man in an airplane flying no more, events from the future or events from the past, the energy surrounds us and will always last. Life is an illusion, memories are too, all you have to do is realize this, and there isn't anything that you can't do.

4-1-2000
A New World

Life is a choice, it's just a game that we play, and we have been playing it for centuries, but we always play the same way. We have been brainwashed for eons from father to son, we have been brainwashed for centuries, each and every one.

Make new beliefs, that's what we have to do, make new choices and this planet will come along too. We can still save this planet, but it's entirely up to you, because this all involves the choices that you choose. Your beliefs are your world that you create every day, and if you change your beliefs, your world will change today.

1-27-01
A Normal World

Domestication and the power you have are yours alone in this world gone mad. This world is but an illusion and so are you, you have the ability to create anything you have the desire to do.

Domestication and the way you were raised is the power you have, it's the power you made. A normal world is filled with higher energy, and a normal world can be created by you and me. Normal isn't normal, it's only normal for you, and that's the "GLITCH" in this plan they want us to use.

We are not computers that you can program every day, each one has his or her own problems and solutions that he or she creates in many different ways.

5-10-03
A Seconds Thought

The energy from the Universe: this is who I really am, the rest is an illusion that was created by man. My looks may differ from day to day because of my thoughts or what I have to say. I have created my life the way I wanted it to be; by choosing my choices, this became my reality.

I've been here fifty-two years of what we call time, fifty-two years or a second's thought of the mind. Time is energy, energy is time, and time, it only exists in one's own Mind.

A Thing of the Past

Age is a number that doesn't really exist, and time is the place where we created all of this. Time doesn't exist either; it's only a state of mind, it's a belief that we have created and create all the time.

You created Santa Clause when you were a child and spooks and goblins under the bed for just a little while, you grew up, you changed in many ways, and they became a thing of the past as they are today.

Time waits for no man, because it doesn't exist, and throughout time we created all of this.

2-11-2000
A Time to Remember

I love this life, I love the things that I can do, and all I have to do is remember, because I've done them all before, I've done them through you. The Past, Present and the Future, they're all happening at their appointed times, only on different plains and dimensions and different outcomes of the mind.

Remembering the Future isn't that hard to do, because you've already been there and done that, it isn't anything new. The Future is like a present that you can unwrap at any time, all you have to do is remember, and the Future is yours and mine. If you don't remember the Future, the Past will repeat itself, and the World will go dormant for you and everyone else.

9-8-96
A Better Man

I feel confident with my life, I chose who I wanted to be, I chose my parents, and I chose my sexuality. My life always changes, there are lessons to be learned at each and every corner, that I choose to make a turn.

The pain in my life is some guilt trip that I have been put on by something that has happened or something that has gone wrong, get rid of the guilt and the pain will soon be gone, keep repeating affirmations and your body will grow strong.

Every pain and every symptom that life is taking you through is brought about by some past experience life has taking you to.

I appreciate my life and just who I am, and with each and every day of my life, there comes a better man.

3-8-2000
Alien

I have written this in the future, but I live here in the past, with a ton of players in my program that just seems to last, and last, and last. Each one I have come in contact with is a brother from the STARS that hasn't evolved enough on this planet yet to know just who they are .

We came here in the future to colonize this star, but over the millennium a few of us forgot just who we are. Our bodies are different, so we had to change our form, and in doing so, we have lost all contact with the Universe in which we were born. I am waiting for the miracle of evolution to come around, so they will finally realize that we are all just visitors on this planet that we have found.

I live in the now, the present time where nothing can happen unless it enters the mind. Time has no meaning for people like me, unless you desire or want it to be. The physical body isn't really a form, it's just an illusion that you have had since you were born. You have been domesticated with this thing that we call the world plan, and it's time to open your eyes and become your own man.

Energy is like a river that flows, it keeps getting stronger with this planet we know. Mother earth is calling, father time is too, but time doesn't exist unless you want it to. The choice is yours, the future is too, this world could be beautiful but only if you want it to.

3-26-02
Always Now

I feed on the information that I choose to receive into this computer that I call me. I created the oceans, I created the seas, I created this world, and then I called it me. Everything that you do, everything you see, you created out of love for people like me.

7

Vibrations are energy, and energy is what you are, the energy in this universe that's in each little star. Time passes each and every day, but the time is now, always. The minute, the time, the second too, the hour of the day, they were all created by you. The creation of the universe happened on its own, or are we responsible for creating the unknown?

2-5-97
America

America is becoming a mountain that you can't climb with all the violence and crime going on all the time. It makes you want to just crawl into a hole, where you can be safe and all alone.

America isn't a bit like it used to be, home of the brave and land of the free, you have to keep locks locked on your door, or you won't have what you had the night before. Whites, Blacks, it's still the same, no one wants to admit it, but it's still the same old game. Come on, people, we have got to make our stand, if we want to make this country into a better land.

12-10-2000
Angels

Angels are among us, it doesn't really matter who, because an angel is someone who will help you in spite of the things that you do. Angels are with us, take the guy down the street, begging for food or something to eat. Angels come in all shapes and forms, and an angel was with you the day you were born! Knowing isn't knowing, reality isn't real, you create up on this planet by the way that you feel. Feelings are energy, good or bad, and they create the things that you have or had. We are all but energy each and every one, we are all but energy from under the sun. We are brothers and sisters, it doesn't matter who you are, because we are the energy from throughout the stars.

12-30-96
Another

Put one after another, that's just the way it's got to be. Put one after another, you can do it, and you can do it for me. Put one after another, you can do it tonight, put one after another, and everything will be all right.

Time was when you didn't understand, but the time is born to every man. Life is easy to figure out when you know your mission and what life is all about. Time has come today, I know who I am, my days of running are over, and this is where I'll make my stand.

5-18-96
Antichrist

In the year 2039, the third and final Antichrist will come into his prime.

He'll wage war on every man, woman, and child, and the Earth will shake for just a little while, on May 5 of that year, the Antichrist will first appear.

The Earth will tremble for the next twenty-five years or until the comet does appear, which will mark the beginning of the end for mankind and all of his friends.

Look into the past for a cure to avert this travesty, and all my words will disappear.

1-12-97
Aquarius

I'm an Aquarius, I've always gone my own way, I've never really cared what other people think or say. They say we're all dreamers, but the world doesn't understand, what the world needs now is the dreamer that's born in every man. The inventors were dreamers that focused on their own plan to make this world a better place for each and every man.

Some people call us eccentric, because we won't conform, we won't do things in a certain way that other people consider the norm. Thank God for the dreamers, because they're the ones who will change this world for the better for each and every one.

7-27-96
Arthur

To the west of England in the far distant past, there was a man called Arthur who came to power at last. It was the fifth century when Rome left to conquer other lands, when this man came to power to rule with an iron hand.

He brought democracy to this land, and rulers in later years would declare kinship to this man. He was born in Glastonbury near the shores of Tripoli and raised by Merlin, the magician in the fifth century. He brought the power to this land with a sword called Excalibur that he wielded in his hand.

He died in battle with a mortal wound, and Camelot died with him all too soon.

7-15-01
Ashes to Ashes

Ashes to ashes, dust to dust, we are all the same, each and every one of us. No death on this planet, you create who you desire to be to experience life and this thing that we call energy. We are all energy is what I am trying to say, this illusion of life is just a game that we have decided to play.

You created the heavens, you created the stars, you created the love up on this planet, and you created who you are! The future is the present, the present is the past, what goes around comes around, and the now will always last.

Surrender to the moment, surrender to the time, surrender to this life force and enter the mind. The life force of this planet is the energy within, and as soon as we realize this, our journey can begin.

3-24-2000
Atonement

Everything exists within your mind, reality belongs to you. You create your impossible dream by choosing the choices you choose. Everything normal and everything weird, you created by choices, so why should you show "any fear?" The impossible dream, it's waiting for you, all you have to do is make the right choices, and that dream can come true.

The second coming that so many people fear is really the Atonement that we have all been waiting for for all of these years. When peace and love are shared across this land and there isn't a single being that doesn't understand.

8-30-03
Brothers Forever

Brothers forever, brother of mine, brothers in this life, the next, and through time. The choices are out there for you and me, the choices that are out there make up our destiny. We can follow whichever road we choose, but it still comes back to me and you. They say that blood is thicker than water, but that just isn't true, the world is an ocean, it all depends on the wave you choose.

Mountains, forests, rivers, and streams, this world is energy, and without that, life doesn't mean a thing.

12-3-96
Ball of Light

I'm a spirit, a ball of light, nothing but pure energy, I animate this body I'm inside of, so it takes care of me. I have all the answers but none of the experiences life can take me through, so with each body that I enter, there's always something new.

I've gone by many names, I've had many lives before, this life will take me through some experiences that I haven't explored. When this body deteriorates as they all seem to do, I'll just find another body and start life anew. The experiences I've had throughout the centuries are experiences that I can truthfully say have happened to me.

6-29-97
Beauty

There is no such thing as beauty, beauty is only in the mind. Beauty is in the eye of the beholder, and it's been there for such a long time.

Beauty is the personality, the perceptions of the mind, beauty is all of these things wrapped in one until the end of time.

You might have a disability, you might just be one of a kind, but you have that special beauty inside the spirit and the mind.

One day, the world will realize that we are all just one of a kind, and we can all start living the way we should with spirit instead of the mind.

Beliefs

Beliefs are something that are taught to you by someone who respects and cares about the things that you do. They're kept deep down in your heart where no one can touch them or take them apart. They keep getting stronger each and every day until they become part of your life in every way.

I'm an instrument from the man above, I write about what he tells me, and I write about love.

6-18-2000
Believe in Yourself

Life is an illusion that you create all of the time every single day of your life, you're creating all of the time. Your beliefs become your reality, it's a simple thing to do, all you have to do is believe, and your desires all come true.

Feelings are energy, beliefs are too, and you create energy when you believe in you. Believe in yourself, that's what you have to do, believe in yourself, and this world will come along too!

The energy from this planet, the energy from the stars, the energy from the universe will show you just who you really are.

9-30-2000
Believe that You Know

This world's messed up, but it's always been that way because of the people and the things that they say. It's an ego trip, "I'm the best in the land," but really they're no better than any other man! Insight and inspiration are all that you need, and it's a power that's built inside of everyone, even you and me! Using this power isn't that hard to do, but first, you have to believe that it's inside of you. Knowing and believing, it's all the same, but the word, that's the "BIG" drawback in this little game.

The ego trip that other people are on will always put you down and keep telling you you're wrong. There is no wrong or right, so what do they know? It's only your beliefs that keep you on the go.

11-29-03
Believing Is Seeing

Believing is seeing, and seeing becomes true, this planet is energy, and it belongs to me and you. The colors, the oceans, the colors, the trees, this is all imagination and was created by you and me. Love comes in many shapes and forms, we create the energy, and love is born. The love of a child, the love of a toy, the love of each little girl and boy.

Death, destruction, the negative side, with this on our planet, no one survives. Believing is seeing, and seeing becomes true, this planet is created by me and you.

6-3-01
Beyond the Mind

You create beyond the mind, that's all that you will ever do, but you live within the body, and that defines who's who. Problems arise every now and then, but you have the means and the desire to meet that end.

Take a deep breath, feel it inside, feel the body just come alive, you're in the now, the present time where no problems can exist or enter the mind. You live in the now, and that's all you will ever see, but create beyond the mind, and that's not all you will ever be.

Just a game that we play all of the time, just a silly game that we play with in the mind, it helps you to relax and realize just who you really are, you're the energy of this planet, the, moon, and the stars.

1-30-2000
Big Problems, Little Problems, Problems on a String

My body is dormant, and it will not age, it will not get sick, because it will just get in the way. I was sent here on a mission to define this place and to make it better for the human race. The big problem is what I need, because it won't be invented until 2073. I could invent this, but if I do, it would throw off the evolution of this planet, so what do I do ?

You think it's funny, " I KNOW YOU DO!" You give me all of these problems down here just to see what I'm going to do.

1-1-2000
Bigots

Find what you enjoy, enjoy what you find, and you too can and will empower the mind. Free your mind, and your fondest desires can come true, if you free the mind that's inside of you.

Bigoted people, people who want to keep things the same, are the very same people who seem to be holding us back with a tight rein.

The underground of free thinkers, which also includes me, are trying to set the world's population free. We've lost a few battles, but we haven't lost the war. Creativity is upon us, and we'll be back for more.

6-21-99
Black-Knighted Colors

Don't let it come in, don't let it take control, you are the Master or the Mistress of your own ego. The black-knighted colors, the Demons from the past, they were only in your mind, they were never intended to last. They taught you a lesson or two or three, and then they left for all eternity.

The darkness of the night, the colors of the day shed light on this planet in a marvelous way. The energy that flows here belongs to you and me, and it will be ours for all eternity.

10-28-2000
Blinded

My eyes are wide open, but still I cannot see, my senses are heightened in this new reality. I hear sounds that I have never heard before, and the touch of a hand means so much more. Time doesn't matter to me anymore, because time doesn't exist behind a closed door. I visualize the world that I cannot see, and with my mind , this becomes my reality. My eyes are wide open, although I cannot see, this world is what you make of it, and that becomes your reality.

12-2-96
Body and Soul

Time is irrelevant, there is no time, it's just a thought that was placed there in our minds. Earth, Wind, Fire, and Rain, the four elements of life that will never change. The fifth is Ether, which is pure energy, energy of the body that we cannot see.

The spirits in our bodies are nothing but pure energy, they take us through life to form our destiny. Every time we rest, our spirits come forth in dreams to give us clues to our life and show us just what they mean. It would appear, all you have to be is a detective to know what he means by all of these clues that he gives us in our dreams. I'm no detective, and I have no idea of what they "mean," all of these clues he gives me in my dreams.

5-7-2000
Body

I love the human body, it's an incredible machine, it's a work of art, if you can figure out just what it all really means. The colors of an Aura, the blues of the sky, the choices that you choose, and you still have no idea why.

I'm not here to teach you, but I'll just give you one little clue, the first thought that you have is the real you. Call it intuition or insight if you must, but the first thought that you have makes you one of us. The body was never intended to age, the body was never intended to die, but still all of you negative thinkers ask the reason why.

1-13-97
Brother Bob

Today is my brother's birthday, but he died back in '79, he was just thirty-one and entering into his prime. He died in Alaska, down in the Alaskan Bay, at least that's what all the reports I've read seem to say.

They never found his body, so we couldn't bury him like we should, we can't even go to the grave if we're in the neighborhood. All I've got are memories that keep spinning through my mind, memories of my brother that just seem to keep coming up at this date in time.

7-13-03
Circles

Time passes so quickly, but time doesn't even exist, man keeps running in circles, because he created all of this! Domestication, it started years ago, beliefs were made that never seemed to grow old. The energy is out there, and it's for you and me, the energy that's out there is the energy that we breathe.

The flowers, the mountains, the oceans, and the streams, the energy of this planet affects everything. Beliefs change our lives, not always the way we want them to, but beliefs can be transformed into something that we can use. There is no way to destroy energy. Quantum physics has already proven that, you can only transform it, and that's a matter of fact.

2-3-96
Candle

The candle quit burning three years ago, but he's still in my heart, because I love him so.

I'll never forget some of the things that he did, he took care of me when I was a kid. He helped me see right from wrong, so I grew up big and strong.

That old guy meant the world to me, and now all I've got are memories. Someday, I'll be with him, I don't know when, but when that day comes, I'll be happy again.

6-2-98
Candy

You're just like candy, you're sweet as can be, and you, you belong to me. Your eyes are hazel with a little speck of green, and inside of you are all of my dreams.

Dreams that could make us happy, dreams that could set us on fire, dreams that could fill both of our desires. You'll always be there for me to hold, and in my eyes, you'll never grow old.

8-1-95
Washington, D.C.

I've got to get a picture in my mind that I can go to when I'm doing my rhymes. I go to my level every night at home, I've got to figure a way to do it when I'm not alone.

People scare me, they always did, I've hated big crowds ever since I was a kid, but there's a lot of people counting on me, I've got to do this for them, if not for me.

Jim Lozen

11-19-2000
Castle

I can open the door, but I can't let you in, you have to desire before your journey can begin. Knowing isn't knowing, reality isn't real, there is no wrong or right, it all depends upon how you feel. You create with your mind everything that you see, you even created your own reality. The future is gone, the past is too, the moment is now, and it's all up to you!

Think with your actions, move with your mind, the secret is hidden in this new world that you will find. The energy is out there for both you and me, and all you have do is use it, and it will set you free!

The lights in the Castle, they may grow dim, but the spirit inside will remain within.

1-23-2000
Catch 22

With your beliefs, you create this world you live in, you create whatever you do, you create all of your problems, you create whatever happens to you. The Good, the Bad, and the Ugly, we bring it all upon ourselves with the energy from this planet, it's you and nobody else.

You're responsible for this planet, you're responsible for everything that you do, you're responsible for the flow of energy on this planet, and no, that isn't a CATCH 22.

9-12-02
Cecilia

We have grown old together, just you and me, you have given me life for all eternity. Death doesn't matter, it's just part of the game, the energy you've had here will still remain the same.

The lives you've touched, the memories you've made will stay with us until our dying day. Rebirth of this planet, rebirth of the soul, the energy that resides here will never grow old.

I'll find you again here, just wait and see, I'll find you again, because I am you and you are me.

2-11-05
Chakras and Energy

Reality changes, time does too, but time doesn't exist without you. The creation of life, it starts every day, you create everything that you think, do, or say. You've created the time, you've created the day, you've created your life in much the same way.

Chakras and energy, that's all you are, charkas and energy, light from the stars. Chakras and energy, the illusion of time, chakras and energy are just a part of the mind.

3-14-98
Chance

Well, I woke up this the morning with tears in my eyes. I had this dream last night that made me feel funny inside.

People were changing right before my eyes, the transformation was taking place without me, and I couldn't understand why.

Fears of a new beginning, fears in the back of my mind, fears of taking a chance are keeping me here for all time. Changes happen every day, but if you won't take the chance, changes will never come your way.

Paths and choices, choices and change, it's all just part of one big game. In your life, there are paths to walk down and choices to make when they come around.

2-4-01
Change Is Coming

Change is coming every day, change is coming in every way. You have to know when to jump and know when to leap, know when to talk and know when to speak. There are little obstacles along the way that you have created and you will bring into play.

Let your mind alone, let it be free, and you will see the answer, it's as simple as one, two, three. The energy around us is the energy we use, it is positive energy, and it is just a tool. Don't dwell on your problems, don't keep them in your mind, because they will materialize, given enough time.

Change is coming every day, are you ready for the change, or are you going to stay the same way?

11-22-99
Changeling

There was a man a long time ago who changed this World to a Heavenly glow. He was a man just like you and me, but he was a man living his own reality. He made his own choices, he made his own plan, he didn't accept authority from any man. He tried to show us the Energy of this land and the Power of the Universe that's in every man.

PEOPLE wouldn't accept him, PEOPLE wouldn't agree, so they put him to DEATH on Mount Calvary.

2-23-97
Changes

My life has changed in the last two years, I have learned how to find and receive the energy that's always here. I have learned how to delve into my past, and I have learned my mission, the time has finally come at last. Through insight and inspiration from the spirits above, I have learned how to fill my life with nothing but love. This is the reason I was brought back here to experience and learn these lessons before I disappear.

We've all had changes in our lives, but these changes that have happened to me just seem to have happened overnight. I'll just keep writing because that's what I do, and when the time comes, I'll be ready to come back to you.

3-4-01
Chess Game

My mind is wide open, my eyes are too, about this love that I give to you. What's done is done, it's in the past, the time is now, and this will always last. Life is an illusion that you create as you go, you created all of your wants, needs, and desires, you created everything that you needed to know.

Out of the past and into the present time, you created your own future from within your own mind. Free will and choices, it's all up to you, you created whatever you needed or wanted to do. Life is like a "chess game" that we play all of the time, because it's a game that you play with mind.

5-5-02
Choice and Outcome

The story is within me, I create it as I go, weather outcome or adventure, I just go with the flow. The energy around you is the making of a plan, no mind is the secret, and it's born to every man. The colors of the ocean, the colors of the sea, the colors of this planet, they are all a part of me.

The dream is a feeling, intuition too, because this is the only kind of energy we use. We tell this story every day, and we create this dream in our own way. Choice and outcome, it's ours for all time, choice and outcome, it's yours and mine.

3-23-95
Choices

The choices you make become your destiny in life. I once made me a choice that cost a man his life.

I was in Vietnam, I was just a kid, but that's no excuse for what I did.

The years have gone by since that time, but I still keep reliving it in my mind, if I had time to think and wasn't so scared, there might have been two of us coming out of there.

11-26-2000
Christmas Is Coming

Christmas is coming, Christmas is here, Christmas and Santa Claus, it's that time of year. Everyone is out at this time of year, visiting friends and relatives and drinking their beer. Santa is laboring hard all through the day, building the toys that the kids will break anyway.

"Accident! He did it, not me!" are the sounds that you will hear coming from underneath the Christmas tree.

Christmas is coming, and Santa will be on his way, with eight tiny reindeer pulling his sleigh, so put the kids to bed early that night, and they can sleep wide awake and "NO ONE WILL FIGHT?"

I long for the days of Christmas past when all I did was drink beer, watch football, and sit on my ass!

12-28-03
Christmas Morn

Christmas memories from the past are Christmas memories that will always last. A gift from Santa under the tree or the Christmas lights that are shining brightly for you and me. The energy that is around on Christmas morn is the energy of love that we have created, and that's how it was born. It's a shame that it comes but once year, this energy of light that will never disappear.

We just put it away when the day is done, put it away until the very next one. We have been domesticated over time, domesticated into believing that we are not all of one mind.

12-8-96
Christmas

Do you believe in the magic that's around this time of year, it will only last for just one month, and then it seems to disappear.

People helping other people, now that's the way it was meant to be, not just one month a year and only around the Christmas tree. People will only help other people when they know they will get a reward, it's just like a dog begging for candy at your feet on the kitchen floor. It's better to give than receive anyway, it will make you feel good inside, and it just doesn't have to be on Christmas day, if people would be like this every day of the year, this would be a better country, and it would always seem like Christmas around here.

4-4-2000
Churches

You're not quite the "ogre" the churches make you out to be, I love you, "Jesus," it's just you and me! With you by my side, there's nothing I can't do, "I love you, Man, it's just me and you." You help me with my writing, you help me with each word that I say, with you by my side each and every day.

I know that the "Devil" is our creation, he is something that doesn't exist, but in the minds of our people, he'll always be a big part of this! We were sent here to create a world filled with love, and it's time we started doing just that, but we're going to need a little help from the "Big Guy" above.

11-20-2000
Cycles

The ultimate life force, the energy that flows belongs to our ancestors from so long ago. We are just dust particles blowing in the wind, and that is how our story begins. Life begot life, we are all one, brothers and sisters under the sun.

Time doesn't matter, the present is the past, the future is now, because the energy will always last. Every minute that passes, every hour of the day, you step into the future, and the past has gone away. Your body is dormant, it's just a tool, the energy within is all you ever need to use. This planet runs in cycles, which isn't that hard to see that this planet is also part of you and me!

Care for this planet as if it were the child you have back home, and care for this planet until it is fully grown.

4-14-95
Civilization

I was off down the road on this cold, rainy day, wondering about life in this world of today.

People killing people, it happens every day, they want something you have, they just pull a gun and take it away.

Times are getting tough on a lot of people out there, they have no job or money, and they just don't care.

7-27-
Co-Creator

I believe in myself and who I am, I believe in this world, but there are just so many people who don't understand. Beliefs are what make this world go around, you get enough people together thinking one way , and that belief becomes a reality in this world of today.

Look at the Bible, it's been revised so many times to fit the current situations of the planet, it boggles the mind.

There is no devil, there is no hell, it's all a belief the church gave you to keep you under their spell. When the people realize what the hell is going on, we can change this planet for the better before something else goes wrong.

Coin

I'm considered a freak to my peers, but little do they know I've been this way for years. There was a time when I was like them, putting down everything I didn't understand, because I thought I was a real man.

I wasn't born this way, something happened to me, and I'm glad it happened, because it set me free.

Handicapped people trust in everyone, big mistake, because normal people just trust in number one.

They're messing up our World, and there's nothing we can do, because we're all handicapped, and they think we're idiots too.

They put us in homes and institutions and such, because they say they've had enough, well, we've had enough too, and in the end, the handicapped people will be back again.

11-3-2000
Colors of the Sun

Energy is a feeling, energy is a mood, negative or positive, it's all up to you. In negative thinking, we have colors that are gray, colors that are black or dark, colors that just seem to fade away.

The secret is in your Aura, the Aura is your soul, the so-called Garden of Eden in days of old. Positive thinking keeps us right there with the vibrant colors that are everywhere.

Yellows, greens, violets, and blues are just some of the colors that will come to you. This may sound like I'm crazy, this may sound like I'm out of my mind, but these energy colors work, and they work all of the time.

5-5-97
Colors

I have to focus on the subject, the subject at hand. Focus on the subject, or I don't understand. I can see all these colors in my mind, some people call them Auras, but I still see them all the time. All I have to do is focus on some person, place, or thing, out in the sunlight then the colors they will bring. People are different colors at different times of the day, dark green turns to light green as the energy fades away.

The color of my spirit, the color of my soul, the colors on this planet just seem to make my energy flow. Energy is out there, for each and every man, all you have to do is use it before you begin to understand.

6-22-03
Come Along

Free your mind and come along with me to the far reaches of possibility. Everything is possible given enough time, everything is possible in one's own mind. We created the universe, we created the stars, we create as individuals, it doesn't matter who we are.

You created your own life the way you wanted it to be, and you will create your own death, because this is your reality, but you won't die, your energy will still live on in the mountains, the forests, and even the little bird singing his song.

1-5-97
Come Together

We have to come together, we have to settle down, we have to learn to love one another, because the twenty-first century is coming around. The world is divided, so we have to make a plan, we have to come together to join in every man.

United, we stand, divided, we fall, we have to come together soon, or it will be the end of us all. John and Paul, they said it the best, "Love is all you need," and God will do the rest. He helps you through insight and inspiration whenever he can, all you have to do is pick up on it to be a better man.

Help each other, if you can, that's how it starts, that's where the road began. If you can't figure that out or if you can't understand, you'll never be that better man.

1-18-97
Come with Me

If you ever come with me, I'll change your world so you can see. I'll show you the energy that abounds, and I'll teach you to see the Auras that are all around. I don't have much money, but that's one thing I don't need, because the energy of the mind, it sets me free.

Thought waves like radio waves, they can be found, it's out in the Universe where they abound, it's just like channeling, you let your mind go, and the energy will begin to flow.

It will be seen in my lifetime, that man learns to harness the energy of the mind. The year will be 2021 when the age of Aquarius has finally come. A new revolution, a revolution of the mind will come to the world as it starts to unwind.

2-18-01
Common Bond

We have one thing in common, you and me, we both share this planet's life-giving energy. Everything else, it's up to you, whatever you have and whatever you do. This life is an illusion, it's pretty cut and dried, what you think you feel inside.

Your mind is a computer with memories of the past, all of your judgments that you have made and the experiences that you have had. There is no Devil, and there is no Hell, "God" is the life force of this planet that we know so well.

There is no right, and there is no wrong, it's the feeling inside that will make you grow strong. What's right for you isn't always right for me, it all depends on the energy you receive. Knowing isn't knowing, it all depends on you and the energy that you put forward in the things that you do.

4-25-03
Commune with the Future

Commune with the future, commune with the past, energy doesn't dissipate, it always lasts. Different dimensions, different times can all be brought together by the touch of an object in one's own mind. You can't die, you can only transform, your energy has been here since before you were born.

Reincarnation, lives from the past all come together and will always last. The breeze from tomorrow is the breeze from today, because the time is now and will be always.

3-15-97
Confused

When you're down and so confused and you really have nothing to lose, take a little tip from me and get out there and breathe in some energy. You can find it beneath the trees, just waiting for you and people like me.

It's out there, and one day, the world will see, it's the only power that you will ever need. It will take you by the hand and lead you to the promised land. It will give you insight and intuition from above and give you ideas that you never thought of.

Energy is the only power that you will ever need, energy from the flowers and the trees. This world will be a better place when man learns to harness the energy from his own space.

6-20-95
Fry Cook

Working in a diner since I was eighteen, cooking grits and fries and just a little bit of everything.

I've had a hard life, living on minimum wage, but I've got a few things on the side to supplement my pay.

I've got to work my whole lifetime for this kind of pay, because I can't afford to put any away.

6-15-02
Cookie Jar

The choices I make the things that I do, I owe them all, I owe them all to you. You taught me the lessons, you taught me the rules, you taught me I could do anything, because you are me, and I am you. Starting over, the dream of mankind, starting over is just one step backward, backward in time. Time is irrelevant, time doesn't even exist, we are the ones who started all of this.

Positives and negatives, that's all we are, a zillion numbers in one big cookie jar. This planet we live on isn't quite as it would seem, this planet we live on is just one giant book of dreams.

3-3-02
Cool Thoughts

I am you, and you are me, together we create our very own reality, with these thoughts running through our mind, we are creating all of the time. We are all energy, there is no way to destroy us, we will always be. Domestication of mankind was the dream of this planet and will be until the end of time.

The animals of this planet, they seem to know that time doesn't exist, they just go with the flow. The energy is out there for you and me, together we can create such a beautiful reality.

11-7-98
Cops

They work all night, and during the daytime too, they work on holidays, our boys in blue. They defend the city from all sorts of crimes, and they will do this until the end of time.

They've lost their power over the years, and lost some respect too, because it just seems to have disappeared. Putting their life on the line and not knowing if they're coming back is a pretty scary thought to have all of the time. They do their job the best they can, that's why our boys in blue are the best in the LAND.

2-13-98
Creation

Creation, it starts deep within your mind. When you begin to think, you begin to design. We've had this ability since the beginning of time, and we are just beginning to use the power of the mind.

The energy of this planet and the power of the mind, the universal consciousness work together to help you to design. It doesn't really matter what we think or what we do, because we all have this power, it's born inside of you.

5-28-97
Creativity

Anything I do, I do on my own, anything I create, I do that all alone. My mind is my world, I see things in a different way, I see things as they could be instead of as they are today.

Anything we want, anything we need, all we have to do is think it to create the energy. We created this world and the way it is today, we created this world by the thoughts we think every day. God created the planets and the stars up above, and he created this planet so we could share our love.

3-11-2000
Creator

I am the co-creator of this planet, I was sent here from the stars to teach the people of this planet who and what they really are! The window of the Universe isn't really that hard to see, because the window of the Universe is really you and me.

The trip through the Universe is taken through the mind, and with this, you can unleash the powers of mankind. The power will lay dormant until the one appears, the one who will lead the people of this planet without showing any signs of fear. He will know the secrets, the secrets of mankind, the secrets that were buried away in the far reaches in the valleys of the mind.

1-23-96
Cripple

I've always been a loner, done everything by myself. I've never needed anybody or anybody's help, but those days are gone now, I'm getting kind of old.

I'm all messed up inside now, I'm a cripple, and I'm only forty-five years old.

The doctor, he can't help me, he says there is no cure, this pain is going to get you at least once a year. The days get longer when it strikes, the pain, it's there both day and night.

6-13-96
Critical Mass

The time is right, I can see it in my mind, the people of the Earth will come together in a critical mass of some kind.

It will be a spiritual learning, a joining of the minds, the people of the Earth will come together if they're given enough time.

We will start to work together for the good of mankind when we all come together in this critical mass of some kind.

1-1-99
Crystal

The power of the Crystal is the power of the mind, it's just a tool with which to focus, to go back to a previous lifetime. The white light that you enter with will abruptly change to blue, and then before you know it, there's another person inside of you.

This life that is within was once on the other side, and they're about to take you on one HELL of a ride. It's just like watching *THE TWILIGHT ZONE*, because it's so hard to believe , but all of this is written down in the ANNUALS of Natural History.

5-14-2000
Decisions and Choices

We complete this World, just me and you, with whatever decision we decide to choose. Our lives are different, but we are all the same, we are one with this planet, it's just one big game.

We are one with the oceans, we are one with the trees, we are one with the flowers, and one with the breeze. We are all but energy is what I am trying to point out, we are one with this planet, and that's what it's all about. Every genetic creature that is upon this planet Earth is part of the energy force, for whatever that's worth. Our reality changes from day to day, and this World will change too, but only if you want it that way.

3-27-97
Dated Soul

I'm a dated soul, a spirit inside this body that I occupy. I've seen the world from inside, I've been back again a thousand times to have the experiences I have learned, to know right from wrong in every turn.

The messages, they come from above through intuition and God's love. These are the words that I convey through my writing and everything that I say. The time has come for all of mankind to reach out and touch each other's mind.

We can do this, please understand that the critical mass was born again and has entered our land.

1-7-01
Day's End

What you think, you create, what you create, you feel, the illusions of the mind seem so very real. Positive thinking, it works the same way, but negative thinking, it will kill you one day. Sins of the father, sins of the son, it's the negative factor that's born to everyone.

Be like the water that flows down the stream, or be like the ocean that ferries your dreams. They never stop running, at times they may slow down, but they will never give up, and they will always be around.

The time is now, the future is at hand, all you have to do is make the right choice, and you will begin to understand. As the daylight falls and the darkness sets in, another chapter of your life begins.

3-30-99
Déjà Vu

Everything that is happening has happened before, it's like déjà vu because it's happening once more. You choose what will happen just like you chose it before, so you can relive the same experience that you had before. It's like a drug, it's like a high , because this time it makes you feel so much alive. After it's done, after it's through , you realize you did what you had to do.

Life is a choice for any man, you can be rich or a pauper, do you understand ?

5-13-95
Death

God gave us all a purpose for being here, what it is isn't always too clear. We're all made out of energy, and you can't destroy that, you might die today, but tomorrow, you might be back.

Now I believe in heaven, and I believe in hell, but what I don't believe in is what all those churches tell.

7-8-2000
Death's Doorway

Death is but a doorway to the windows of the mind, that will take you on an incredible journey of an entire life time. The lifetime you are observing is the lifetime of your past, when reality didn't matter and the future was always going to last. Knowing is remembering, believing is too, you have to know to remember, which is also part of you.

Time doesn't matter, it's only in your mind, and rules don't exist, they're only for mankind. We are all just spirits blowing in the wind, and we create whatever we desire on just one little whim. Remember that's all we really have to do, just remember and all of this power will rise up inside of you.

We are all just spirits, spirits of the mind trapped in these bodies until we remember the potential of mankind.

8-2-97
Debbie

You are my sun, my moon, and the stars up above, you are the only woman that I am ever thinking of. I think about you night and day, and as time passes, I know I'll always feel this way. I visualize your face in everything that I see, I visualize our life together and how it was meant to be, and it doesn't really matter if we grow apart, because I'll always keep you right here in my heart.

The days may turn into months, the months, they may turn into years, but as long as I have your love, I will always be here. We can grow old together, just you and me, living life to its fullest the way it was meant to be.

12-31-95
Drugs

Drugs will kill you, like they did me back when I was twenty-three.

I had a college education and a college degree, things were looking up back when I was twenty-three.

I had a lot friends who did drugs, you see, and they eventually got to me. I'm still alive, if you want to call it that, I'm living on skid row out of a backpack.

10-26-96
Decisions

The paths of life are the choices you make, so you'd better think twice about the paths that you take. Your destiny is cloudy until that time when you finally make up your mind, it becomes clearer as you focus on the problem at hand and work it out the best you can.

Your decisions are final, that's just the way it is, you can't go back and do over the things that you did. You can't run, and you can't hide, it's all up to you, and you have got to decide.

12-15-96
Deity

He's always out there to help you, he never turns you away. He gives you the tools to work with every single day through insights and inspiration, that's how he does his thing, you just have to be smart enough to know what tools he brings.

He's just like Santa Claus, but he's here every day, you just keep him in the back of your mind where he's safely tucked away. We don't have to see him to know he's really there, we don't have to see him to know he really cares.

7-03-95
Dilemma

Get up in the morning at the crack of dawn, get to the job before the lights go on. When the sun comes up, I build me a mop and start spreading that liquid hot.

I have been roofing for about thirty years, it's time I thought about getting away from here, but if I retire, I won't know what to do, so I just might as well keep working and bringing my money home to you.

1-1-2000
Demon

She drives me crazy, she drives me insane, this little girl without a name. She takes me on a roller coaster of ups and downs, and I'm never the same when she's around. My mind tells me one thing, but my heart tells me two, and I have no idea of anything or what I should do.

Maybe I should just let it go and see if it's just a love infatuation or see if it grows. Love is a demon, it's always beating at your heart, and you never know what to do from the very start.

9-13-98
Desires

I desire this to happen, I desire you to be mine, when I desire things to happen, they just happen, and it's all done through the mind. When you desire a certain thing to happen, you have to set a date in time, or this thing you want to happen could happen a year or two down the line.

Your wants, your needs, your life's dreams, they can all come true, all you have to do is desire, and they will all come to you.

7-27-02
Desolate Planet

Desolate planet, desolate plain, negative energy, it's all the same. Whatever you do, think, or say, negative energy works that way! Life is an illusion, energy is king, and if we can't realize this, it doesn't mean a thing. The planet, the universe, it's starting to fight back in the only way it can, it's a matter of fact. Reds, yellows, blues, and greens, positive colors is all that it means.

Positive energy will always win out over bad, and negative energy is what this world of ours has.

3-17-96
Destiny

Isn't it weird, the way life works out? There's always a plan that you know nothing about. This plan is called destiny, the man upstairs plans each life out for you and me.

He gives you different roads that you can go down, but he knows which one you're going to take when that part of life comes around.

So there's really not much you can do, just roll with the punches and see what life has in store for you.

3-2-97
Devil

There is no devil, there is no Hell, Hell is on Earth, and most people, they make it oh-so-well. It's a negative world that we're all living in, and the negative thoughts, they just seem to creep right on in.

You have to relearn everything as you did before, relearn everything before you can open up that door. Energy is out there, it's just waiting to be found. Energy from the trees, the flowers, and the energy that's all over the ground. Thoughts will kill you, beliefs will too, unless you can control the energy that's inside of you.

When the door is open, the beauty that you will find, it will just seem to open up your mind. The emotions are there, they will help you to unwind and fill you with love for all of mankind.

12-17-99
Different Dimensions

Time doesn't exist, it's only in your mind, the future and the past are happening *now* at this present point in time. Different dimensions, different wave forms in time, they are just there to guide you through the valleys of the mind.

Life is but a moment for each man, woman, and child. Life is but a dream that will last for just a little while. When the dream is over, another life comes true at some other place in time, this other life is you. The Bible is filled with codes, secrets of the mind that man has tried to cover up for an entire lifetime.

4-21-02
DNA

This world's just an illusion, a quantum leap, and it's full of all the energy, the energy you seek. Interrogator, intimidator, aloof and poor me, these are just four of the many energies. Quantum physics proved this, the illusion is you and me, we are nothing but pure energy.

Electrons and neutrons, DNA codes, we have been here since days of old, energy just can't be destroyed, it's always present in every little girl and boy. The energy of this planet, the flowers and the trees, the oceans and the rivers, they are all part of me. We are all one, it's plain to see that we are all one in this world of energy.

4-24-02
Domestication and Change

Domestication, age, and time only exist if I choose to make them mine. The creation of this planet, the creation of time all started out in one's own mind. Your creating every moment of every single day, you're creating with things that you think, do, or say.

Time is irrelevant, time doesn't even exist, domestication started all of this. We were domesticated since the day we were born, domesticated into this life that we have worn. You can change this, it's only a dream, you can change this because life isn't as it would seem.

7-30-2000
Domestication

Years ago when I was small and didn't have any responsibility at all, I was happy just to be alive, my ma and dad fed me, and that's how I survived. Domestication finally came when I got a little older and could play their game.

They started filling me with all of their beliefs, and I really didn't have a choice, so I got no relief. The day finally came when I was fully grown, and I still had to play this game, because I was out on my own. I raised my family the way they raised me, because that's all I knew, it was part of my life's history.

7-16-2000
Don't Take This Personally

Don't take this personally, because this is only in their minds, we create our own reality and have done so all of the time. We created everything on this planet, we create everything that we do, we create our own problems, and we even created you. Live your life to the limit, all miracles start in the mind with your imagination and a little help from mankind.

Life is but a movie, and you are the star, you create whatever happens, and you create who you really are. Villains, heroes, they are all the same, you created this individual in this one weird little game. Life is beautiful, it lets you create who you want to be and take this individual throughout life's history.

10-8-98
Don't Look Back

Don't look back, it will only cause you Sorrow, look for today, or better yet, look for tomorrow. I Love myself and what I can do, I wouldn't change my Life, not even for you.

Anything I want, anything I need, I just Desire, and it becomes reality. The future isn't certain, it can be changed, all you have to do is set your mind, and it can all be rearranged. Given enough people, we could all set our minds on just one thought and change this World for our entire lifetime.

7-03-95
Dooms Day

Something's happening, something's going on, I don't quite understand it, but something's going wrong.

The good days are behind us, the bad days are still ahead, something has to change, or pretty soon, we're all going to be dead.

Greed and corruption, that's what's going on, we have got to stick together, or pretty soon, we're all going to be gone.

11-18-2000
Doomed

We are all one regardless of your name, regardless of your predicament we are all the same. We have been domesticated for thousands of years to develop on our own until the oneness just disappeared.

The future is now , the time has come for all of this energy to become as one. We need a plan, an idea or two, something that we can all focus on, something that we can all use. I'm not here to teach you, I am just a tool to develop the energy that you just don't seem to want to use.

Colors across the universe, colors across the land, the colors are the energy, but the people just don't seem to understand. I'm here to enlighten, but it looks like I'm doomed, because the negative energy will consume!

8-17-96
Door

I broke on through to the other side on April 8th of '95, the side of enlightenment where everything is alive, most people just see one side of the door, I see both and so much more.

I see things as they ought to be instead of as they are, my Shaman is here, and He guides me through everything I think, say, or do

He helps me with my writing, guides me through each step, reminds me of things that happened so I'll never forget, now it breaks my heart when I have to leave, but he says it's not my time, so I'll just visit every chance I get, there in the back of my mind.

1-31-99
Dragon Master

Fighting the Dragon, showing no fear is the only way that you will ever get out of here. Changing the World for just one man, changing the World, if you can. Fighting the Dragon on his own ground is the only way that you will ever bring him down.

The Dragon, he's all powerful as he takes to the skies, this mighty beast that puts fear in men's eyes! All generations have had them, down to the very last man, you have to Master your Dragons before you can save our land.

6-17-96
Dreams

I had this dream , in the last night or two , I can't get it out of my mind , because it was about you.

I should have told you about it, it might have put you on your guard, and then you might not be laying wear you are.

Dreams have meanings, or so I have been told, I have to put this dream behind me, because I have to let you go.

4-28-02
Experience the Love of Life

Experiences are all in your mind, and you can have them whenever you want at any given time. Your desires are natural, your wants are too, whatever you create is brought to you. We create every moment of every single day in whatever we do, think, or say.

Time doesn't exist, we created that too, time is a belief that we all decided to use. Imagine your life the way it could be, now look at what we have created for you and me. Love is the answer, love is the key, now experience life the way it was meant to be.

9-19-99
Earth Plain

I wish I could write my feelings down on paper, as the words, they flow through my pen, but feelings are energy, and energy never ends. You can't destroy it, you can't even put it out of your mind, because energy is here and will stay here until the end of time.

The people who have died here aren't really dead, you see, because the people who have died here are also energy. Energy surrounds this planet, energy upholds and binds, energy will always be with us until the end of time.

The flowers, the trees, the ocean, and the breeze, he's always with us and always will be.

By Jim Lozen

12-5-99
Earth's People

I love my life, I love what I can do, I love my life, and I owe it all to you. You're the Solar Winds around me, you're air that I breathe, you're the atoms and neutrons that are inside of me. Mother Earth is a life form, the Rivers are her veins, the Oceans are her lungs of life, the Mountains and the Rains.

The Rains, they nurture this planet, help to make it grow, and the trees and flowers on this planet help the energy to flow. I'm no

Rocket Scientist or Mathematician too, but I just happen to know that all the help you'll ever need is built inside of you.

2-7-97
Education

So you've got a college education and a college degree, now you think you're something hot, but you're not, and given enough time, you will begin to see. This world is made out of people just like you, and we're all trying to make it through life doing the best that we can do.

People are just like fingerprints, there are no two just alike, we all have our own little problems, and they're as different as day and night, if we could learn to interact and throw our prejudice aside, we could set this world up for one hell of a ride. If we could just love one another and give each person what they need, there's no telling what this world would be like or that we could succeed.

3-30-96
Ego

Have you ever tried doing something you knew you didn't have any business trying to do, if so, you and me have a lot in common, because I've been there too.

I've messed up most of my life, and each one cuts a little deeper just like a knife, you start to think negative thoughts with everything that you do, and let me tell you something, it'll all come true. I've found a little trick to get over that, it's called Meditation, and it will put you back on track.

I go to my level every chance I can, it helps me mellow out and understand that most of this stuff that I try to do is just pure Ego and I don't need this to help me get through.

Life's hard enough in this world of mine, and I don't need my Ego to screw it up half the time.

2-1-97
Eighteen

He died in Nam, he was only eighteen, he gave his life for his buddies and me. He was just a kid, I didn't even know his name, but he gave his life all the same. He was a new kid who just transferred in, and I didn't want to get that close to him, because new people had the habit of checking out, and I didn't need another memory I could live without.

The years have gone by with the passage of time, but some memories, they just won't leave your mind. It doesn't matter what I do, they just keep coming back whenever they want to. I owe my life to the kid who died that day, because he died in such a special way.

6-21-98
Elizabeth

I've never met you, but I know you were here, your offspring in life have made that so clear. The time was right, you did what you had to do, then you left this World longing for you.

Times have changed throughout the years, but I know you're still with us, I know you're still here. You saved my life a long time ago, you were the woman in white who I didn't know.

You came down to me from Heaven above, took my hand, and gave me all your Love.

9-24-2000
Energy Colors

Yellows, greens, violets, and blues, these are just some of the colors that I see in you. The colors of the ocean, the colors of the trees, the colors of this planet, they all produce energy. Black-knighted colors, colors from the past are the negative colors, colors that just seem to last, last, and last.

Positive thinking seems to bring about a change, but the negative colors are still just part of the game. Breathing in reds throughout the day seems to bring back the energy that simply fades away. Yellows, greens, violets, and blues, these are just some of the colors that I see in you.

7-12-98
Energy Flow

I lived my life in chains, I never knew I had the key until that day came, when the energy just came over me. Things, they just started happening, things that I couldn't explain, things to turn my life around so that it would never be the same. There is no wrong or right, no devil in the night, no hell below, just the energy that seems to flow.

Now I live my life in a different way, I live for the energy that I receive every day.

9-15-96
Energy

It's time, it has come today, the energy inside will not fade away. The more I try to stop it, the more it comes, energy abounds out there for everyone.

The world is a powerhouse for mankind, but they won't accept what they can't find. It's an energy field that most people can't see, but it's still out there for people like you and me, tap into it, it will take you far, it will show you your mission in life and just who you are.

I tapped in about a year ago, and it's taught me many things that I didn't know. Energy goes where energy flows, and it will take you where you want to go. Don't question it's power, it comes from deep within, just sit back, "baby," and enjoy the ride.

11-11-2000
Entities

They're just here to help you, these entities from the past, or could it be from the future, because the now will always last. They create with the energy that's inside of you and me, and with this energy, we will begin to see. Open your mind and let them come in, because this is how our future begins.

Jake is a friend of mine, and he's right here, but Jake has been dead for fifty some years, he helps me with my writing and tells me what to say, he also keeps me in a positive mood along the way.

Some people think I'm crazy, some people think I'm insane, but as long as I got Jake, we're still going to play this silly little game.

1-11-98
Era

The changes in your life, they happen almost every day, the question is, will you be ready when these changes come your way. Positive thinking, now that's the way to be, because you produce an aura of Karmic energy.

This light is like a magnet, it brings you everything you need, this light is like a magnet, this Karmic energy. Through holistic healing and the power of the mind, we will become the forefathers of this new era in time.

8-23-96
Eternity

The time is right, you're always on my mind, I want to be there for you until the end of time. People say that there are barriers, but they're only in your mind, we can live as one until the end of time.

All you have to do is come halfway, and I'll do the rest, I'll take you on a journey, which you will find, will be the best. Soon, we'll reach the planets and the stars up above, then we'll enter this land filled with nothing but love. The energy that flows here comes directly from the mind, this is the way God intended for all of mankind.

We'll take a walk amongst the flowers and down by the sea and breathe in all of the energy from the giant oak trees. I've been here before, this is like a second home to me, and I would like to bring you here for all eternity.

12-29-96
Every Man

Pain is power, power is energy, you have to look at it in a whole new light in order to set it free. All the pain in the world bring it to me, because I have learned how to harness it as energy.

Energy is the only power that you need, energy from the Sun, the flowers, and the trees. Pain is such an energy field, but you have to let it go, because if you don't, it will continue to grow. It produces negative thoughts that you don't need, negative thoughts that produce disharmony.

One day, the world will finally understand the power that's born to every man.

12-20-02
Evolution and Time

Ideas are evolution, and evolution is time, but time only exists if you create it in your own mind. You create with every thought, you create with every single day, you created this illusion of life in much the same way. Life has no ending or a beginning too, life is energy that is both me and you.

This world is changing from day to day, the energy of life makes it that way. One thought travels from mind to mind until it becomes reality in a given amount of time. Edison, Ford, and Columbus too, they all had one idea, and it just grew and grew and grew.

12-20-98
Evolution

Down in the JUNGLES, before our time began, lived our Brother's Ancient man. He was highly evolved as he tended this land, our ancient brothers, the one we call man.

There was no survival of the fittest, we were all one, everything that was done was done for everyone. Then something happened, something entered our land, something called GREED, and it affected every man. As he evolved, he deteriorated in time, and this affected every man's mind.

The world was lost, but it came back once more, but if we can't learn from our mistakes, we'll do just the same as we did before.

9-9-96
Evolving

My world is changing, it's not a bit like it used to be. My friends say they can see it in my writing, but it eludes me.

I must be evolving, because the world looks different to me, I'll notice all these colors, and I'll breathe in nothing but pure energy. I notice all these colors circling some people that I know, at first, I thought that there was something wrong with my eyes, because I didn't know. I found out that they are auras that I can see, I just find it kind of hard to believe that the only one who can see them is me.

Changes are kind of scary when it happens to you, especially when you're set in your way and you don't need anything new.

5-13-01
Experience Life

The future is now, time has passed, this world of ours will always last. Love is the answer, love is the key, love is the main ingredient inside of me. The colors of the ocean, the colors of the sea, the colors of this planet are all colors that you desire to see. Relax your mind, let it go free, relax in this world of our so-called reality.

Nothing can happen, this world is but a dream, destiny awaits, or so it would seem. You chose your own life, you choose whatever you desire to do, this world is just an experience, and it's all just for you.

Our bodies are dormant, age is too, this is all something that you will have to choose. I know the secret, the secret is you, and the reality you chose to live with are the choices you choose.

7-5-96
Future

What goes around comes around, our future is buried in the past. The decisions we make today aren't here to last.

Man makes the same mistakes over and over again, and until we get it right, we'll all be back again.

Our mind is the key to the future, but no one can figure that out, they just go about their humdrum lives and think of no one else.

Maybe it's time for the third and final Antichrist to appear, he would get this world back in shape within a couple years, then people would start to think that our future does lie in the past, and we would have to get rid of him to make this world last.

1-23-97
Fairy Tale

Life isn't always a fairy tale, there's some bad things that can happen to you. Focus on your problems, and intuition and insight will help to see you through. Live by my motto, live by my creed, I've been doing this since '95, and good things have just seemed to happen for me. Positive thinking, that's what you need, and you can get that positive energy from the colors or the trees.

Imagine a world, if you can, where life isn't a problem for any man, no race, no color, no prejudices of any kind, this is the kind of world I would like to see in my lifetime.

By Jim Lozen

1-16-2000
Father

Thank you, father, for you are me, thank you, father, for sharing your wisdom and letting me see. Comes a time in every man's life when he isn't sure of what's wrong or what's right. Then it just dawned on me that there is no wrong or right, everything is as it should be.

The nature of this planet, the colors of the streams, if you look deep within yourself, you will know just what I mean. The destruction of this planet are from the choices that we made, if we make different choices, this planet could make a comeback, and it could start today.

10-17-97
Fear

Good and evil, evil and bad, there is no evil, only the fears that we all have. The fear of dying, the fear of being alone, the fear of not having a place to call home .

Pain and fear, fear and pain, they go together, because they're both the same. Pain is not knowing what's going on or what's going to happen or what's going wrong.

The fear of dying, of letting go, of unfinished business from so long ago. Let go of this fear, this fear is nothing at all, the fear of dying and going into another dimension is waiting for us all.

8-19-96
How Does It Feel

How do you feel when you're all alone, when darkness comes and you're on your own?

How does it feel on them lonely nights when the people you love are out of your sight?

The sun sets in the West, and darkness comes in, there's nowhere to go, and there's nothing to win, so how do you feel when you're on your own and darkness comes and you're all alone?

7-18-99
Field of Dreams

Anything that I desire, anything that I want to do, I just put my mind in motion, and it's there in front of you. I don't know how I do this, if I did, I couldn't explain, but the mind is energy, and to me, it's all the same.

You're here for a purpose or a mission, so it would seem, to put your two cents into the field of dreams. If I could get just one person to feel the same way that I do, feelings are the energy that keeps growing inside of you.

11-3-02
Fifteen Years

You gave us your knowledge, you gave us our dreams, you changed a few lives, or so it would seem. The door lies open for every man, but so few take it, because they just don't seem to understand.

Fifteen years of fighting, fifteen years of defending our own, fifteen years with Walter Stonebridge, fifteen years of this place that we called home. You might have been just one little ripple in time, but the memory of you will last forever in our own minds.

As one door opens and another shuts tight, we will meet this challenge in a brand new light.

2-2-96
Old Flame

I can't stay here very long, I should leave before something goes wrong.

Times aren't like they used to be, I don't want you, and you don't want me, if this happened just a few years ago, I might have had a change of heart, I don't know.

You say you love me and you'll be true, but you've said that before, how do I know I can trust in you? You've broken my heart a few times before. I can't take the chance, and I won't open the door.

10-27-96
Flashbacks

Flashbacks are something that I'll never understand, I'll never know if they really happened or if they made me who I am.

Memories are a priceless thing, it's part of growing old, but I'm missing four months out of my life from such a very long time ago, it happens every now and then, I'll go back in time to be with some friends, we're all sweating from every pour, and then a bright light comes, and there's nothing more.

I wish I knew what happened on that date in time, and then maybe I would stop reliving this thing in the far reaches of my mind.

2-17-01
Fluid Motion

We have done this in the future, we have done this in the past, we are going to do this once more, and the moment will always last. The future is uncertain, the past is too, but all of these times, they are already inside of you. Your choice decides your future, and your future is your past, what goes around comes around, the moment will always last.

The morning after sunset, the sunset after dawn, is the moment that you exist in, a world that can't go wrong. You create with your mind, the world that you see, we created this planet and all of humanity. Time doesn't matter, time really isn't here, you create at the moment, and time seems to disappear. What man has created, time will wear away, but time doesn't exist in the world of today.

5-27-2000
Forest Rain

Everyone is the equal of every other man, makes no difference who they are or what they understand. We are one with the oceans and one with the sea, we are one with this life force that we call energy.

Energy is everywhere, it's in each and every thing, energy is upon this planet in the life it seems to bring. The morning dew, the forest rain, a valley at sunset are just a few examples of the energy that we will not soon forget.

The forest rain as it's coming down brings the life force to this planet as it touches ground.

11-21-99
Forgiveness

Colors of a dream, colors you have never seen, colors of the wake of night, colors in the bright sunlight. Colors from ages past, colors that shouldn't last. Demons step right through that door into the present forevermore.

Forgiveness, that's the key, forgive the Demons, then forgive ME! The past, present, and the future, they are all intertwined, they are all happening NOW at this present point in time.

7-9-2000
Four Agreements

The four agreements, the black magic of man that we don't even know about and don't even understand. The word is power, and we use it all of the time, and with these words, we can creep into each other's mind.

Low self-esteem, it's in there too, it's just one of these words that we happen to use on our daughters or on our sons, the word is belief, and it's in everyone. The third is ego, and it's born to every man, the power to corrupt just because he doesn't understand.

The fourth is love, which is what this world is all about, but as long as we have the other three, they will always cancel love out.

6-5-2000
The Fourth Dimension

Time doesn't exist, there's another world that you can't see, and it's just waiting to enter into your reality. In this other world, the sun never dies, it's always shining brightly up in the sky. You can be anything that you wish to be, all you have to do is desire, and it will happen naturally.

Time travel is a thing of the past, because all you have to do "NOW" is think, and you're there in a flash. There aren't any problems in this world of ours, because we have eliminated time to reach for the stars. The fourth dimension is where I'll be, and I'll live in the "NOW" for all eternity.

4-15-2000
Free Will

Nothing happens by accident, it's always the reality that we choose day by day, things that we say, and the illusions that we happen to use. Everything happens for a reason, could be the beliefs that we say or choose, could be the energy that surrounds this planet or the energy that we use.

We are responsible for all of our actions, because they are the choices that we decided to choose, they are the building blocks upon this planet, they are the cornerstones that we just happen to use. I couldn't write this without my own choices and the words that I decided to use, because without free will, I have no choices, and I just do what I am told to do.

8-10-95
Freedom

Freedom isn't free, there's a price you have to pay every time we have to throw a life away.

The jungles of Nam are scary when you walk your patrol late at night, but I flew in a gunship I thought I was all right.

I found out different after about a month or two, we were getting picked off like flies, and there wasn't anything we could do.

One mission I remember getting shot down, I was in Virginia when I finally came around, my buddies, I don't know what happen, and I guess I never will, but that's the price you pay for freedom, and I guess you always will.

4-17-95
Friend

To have a good friend is what life is all about. Friendship is something you just can't live without.

To go through life from day to day without a good friend is a terrible way.

Living life without a good friend isn't living at all, it's the living end.

2-23-2000
Friends for Life

I just had to know what was going on, so I made my move, and it turned out to be wrong. I asked the Big Man for some help from above, and he, in turn, filled my heart with nothing but love.

He stopped the Ego right dead in his tracks, so whenever I'm in trouble, I'll just keep going back. I know now what I should do, I'll just be friends for life, but I'll just go on loving you.

1-30-96
Arthritics

Summer is the time for me, because the pain is gone, it sets me free. I'm arthritic, so when the pain strikes, it hurts so bad, it's there both day and night.

When the summer comes, I'm like a new man, I've got five or six months to do what I can, so I'll try to get everything done, and if the mood hits me, I'll go out and have some fun. When the summer's gone and winter sets in, there's not much I can do, because it's back again.

12-29-98
Generations

He created the PLANET, he created the STARS, he created the PEOPLE, but we create whoever we are. We EVOLVE through lifetimes, each one is our own, we EVOLVE through the Centuries, but we do that all alone. Through Lucid Dreaming, Power Animals, and Crystals of all kinds, we can do anything through the Power of the Mind.

People don't understand this, people don't have a clue, so I am writing this down in the HOPES that it will help you. Tell the future generations the next MAN to appear is the man we have been waiting for for all of these years. He is the Ascents of Energy, the POWER of the Mind, he will show us how to live for all ETERNITY and use the Power of the Mind.

11-12-2000
GHOST

She was hitching a ride just to get back home, it was cold outside, and she was chilled to the bone! We stopped to give her a ride, and Betty Lou told her just to jump inside. She gave her her jacket just to keep her warm as we drove down the street in our Geo Storm.

She gave us an address, and we wrote it down, then she didn't say a word until we got to town. We stopped at the address that we had written down, looked to tell our passenger, but she was nowhere to be found. We walked up to the door to tell the man inside, and he, in turn, told us the story about his newly deceased bride.

A hit-and-run driver had killed his bride, and she was buried down the road at Morning Side. We thought that this was kind of weird but we had better check this story out before we got out of here.

We stopped at the graveyard and looked inside and found Betty Lou's jacket on the gravestone of the man's deceased bride.

1-03-96
I Can't Let You Go

Just because I left you doesn't mean we can't be friends. I have some problems I have to deal with, but then I'll be back again.

You're the only one who's ever meant something to me, I can't imagine life without you or what life would be. I'll be back again someday, I know, because I can't live without you and I can't let you go.

6-26-2000
God's Each and Everyone

I was awaken, but still, I couldn't see the beauty of this planet, for it eluded me. The picture-perfect horizon at the setting sun, the illusions that are born within everyone.

Life is an illusion, you create what you see, you created the colors, and you even created me! I didn't do this writing, it's all in your mind, you created the words that you wanted to find. You create everything that you want to do by just having the thought that's inside of you.

We are all Gods, and our choice was clear, to experience life, we had to come down here.

7-1-04
Goody Miss Two-Shoes

Goody Miss Two-shoes, the queen of the ball, had everything but still had nothing at all. Born into luxury from the start, she had everything except a heart. Goody Miss Two-shoes, queen of the ball, had everything but still had nothing at all.

Domestication had done this to her, she learned everything without saying a word. Domestication, it comes a long way, it came out of the past and right into today.

3-10-95
Handicapped People

Handicapped people have a hard life to do, I should know, because I'm handicapped too. God gave us a gift when he took one away, mine was my writing when I have something to say.

I can't speak too clearly, most people don't understand, they think I'm retarded and try to lend me a hand, I don't need their help though, and it makes me so mad, I'm as good as them or any other man.

12-28-96
Harmony

So many places to go, so many things to do, life just isn't long enough to do everything that I would like to do. I've done everything that I can think of, but all I ever wanted is someone to love. Someone to be with, someone to hold, someone to stay with when I grow old.

I'm just killing time now, really all I do, I'm just killing time now while I'm waiting for you. I don't know if I'll ever find you or if you'll find me, but that's one thing I would love, because it would put my life in complete harmony.

7-29-2000
Hate Sites

Hate sites on the Internet, hate sites all over this land, they're created by little people who don't even understand. They recruit the ignorant people and our children every day, all they have is a big "Ego" that guides them in whatever they happen to say.

All we are is just a spirit, and these bodies are just tools that we chose to get around in and that we just happen to use. We are all just one now, that might be a little hard to believe, but we are all just one in this world that we created and the world that we can see.

There are many different planets, on this one that we call Earth, many different stages of evolution that we call rebirth. God's chosen people, it wasn't just the "Jew," it's everyone on this planet, even me and you.

8-9-98
Hazel

She has big blue eyes, and she stands five-foot-three, this girl is poetry in motion and wants the whole world to see. She has worked her whole life for nickels and dimes and has had to miss out on a lot of good times.

Raising a family on your own, is twice as hard when you're a woman and all alone. A working-class hero is what she is, raising a family, working for a dime, how many women in this world could do this all of the time?

8-6-03
Hell of a Dream

If it wasn't for you, I wouldn't be me, and this wouldn't be my reality. My beliefs are my future, my fears are my past, and anything that I do, I know will always last. This world is energy as far as the eye can see, this world is energy and also you and me. Anything you think, say, or do, it becomes energy, and it was created by you.

The oceans, the mountains, the valleys, and the streams, it's all an illusion, but it's one hell of a dream.

10-20-96
Hell

Sunday night, I'll be with you, Monday morning, I'll be there too. Tomorrow means nothing as long as I'm here with you. We grew up together, we were always side-by-side, without your love, I don't think I could have survived.

Now that it's happened, now that you have died, I don't know what I'm going to do, without you here by my side. The days, they seem so lonely, the nights, they never end. This is just like being in hell, because I lost a very good friend.

1-3-97
Heritage

In the beginning before time began, we were all just part of an energy field, not part of any man. When it all came together and we started to come down, we developed control drama's to get the energy, that couldn't be found.

Man started killing to get the power that he craved, he started killing, and he's still killing today. The energy is out there, it's just something that can't be seen, it's in the trees, the colors, the flowers, and the breeze. The Indians knew this, they still know it today, but the white man won't accept what the Indians have to say.

Man will kill anything that he doesn't understand, that's the heritage that's born in every man.

4-26-99
Higher Power

I love my life, and I love the things that I can do, I love this World now that I found out how to get in touch with you. Each day that passes, each day that I go through is another day that I have that I can spend with you.

I make the choices, but you make the plan, then you give them to me in words that I will understand. The people whom I have talked to, the people whom I have seen are the same people who have been there to fulfill all of my dreams.

I make the choices, but you make the plan, and with you by my side, I will be that better man.

10-31-98
Halloween

The leaves are changing, the North Winds blow, on Halloween, the full moon will show. The Graveyards will all come alive with spirits of the past, and on broomsticks, witches ride! They say this happens but once a year when people just seem to live in fear.

The dogs, they HOWL, people go INSANE, as the DEVIL appears to take all of the blame. The only GHOSTLY DEMONS that will appear that night are about three feet tall, and all they want is just a little BITE.

3-16-02
Honeybee

Love is all around us, love is everywhere you see, love is the making of honey from each little bee. The color of an aura, the color of the sky, the color of midday as the sun passes by. The color of a sunset, the color of the sea, these colors of the planet are all found in you and me.

Love is all around us, love is everything that you see, love is the making of this Planet that we will all but one day see.

9-25-98
Hope

After the War is over and the final battle has already been won, the black-knighted colors will take over the Earth, and it will affect everyone. The Rivers will dry up, and the Black Rains will come, they will last for sixteen years before we see the Sun.

Then the Earth will make a comeback, not right away, but things will just seem to get a little better each and every day. The Rains will come back, the Rivers will begin to flow, and the colors of this planet will begin to grow.

It will be April 8th of that year, Aries will be in Sky, and the disparity will just seem to disappear.

2-7-2000
Horror

One hundred and one, or was it one hundred and three, I don't really remember, because this wasn't happening to me! They came out of the sky, they came straight at me, but this had to be an illusion, it couldn't have been happening to me.

Dark-knighted colors, Demons from the past, I knew this was an Illusion, so I knew it couldn't last. Deep within the valleys of the mind live the Hatreds and the Sorrows of all of mankind. So many things that I can't explain, the clues are in my writing, but to me, they all look the same.

Ten minutes of Horror, and then everything just seems to quiet down, I'm back in my room as the candle is burning down.

4-9-97
Human Race

The night is changing into day, the sky is becoming clearer in every way. The time has come for all of mankind to make the jump into improving his mind. This world isn't a bit like it used to be, when material things were all that you would ever need.

It started out in groups of one or two, and then with the energy, it just grew and grew. The people, they just don't seem to understand that there is a mission born into the life of every man to make this world a better place, to change it for the human race.

4-20-2000
Just Me and You

I love everything about you, I love everything that you do, you're my whole heart and inspiration, I love just being here with you. I spent my whole life trying to find you, I spent my whole life looking for someone just like you, it doesn't matter what you do, babe, because we belong together, just me and you.

We will spend our lives together, time no longer exists for me and you, we will spend eternity together side-by-side, just me and you. This whole world may evolve around us, it doesn't matter what they do, as long as we have each other, that's all we need girl, just me and you.

4-26-98
I Believe

I believe in the sun, I believe in the stars, I believe in the magic that makes you who you are. I believe you create with every thought that you make, with every breath that you take.

I believe in myself, I believe in what I do, I believe in the spirit that's born within inside of you. I believe in the sun, I believe in the stars, and I believe in the people, whoever they are.

11-08-95
Illusion

Life is an illusion, it's all in your mind, you can do whatever you want at any given time.

All you have to do is focus, and we all can do that, focus on anything that's handy wherever you're at.

Clear your mind, let your body be gone, become part of what you're focusing on.

I've been to my level many times before, this helps me to relax and opens that door.

4-19-97
Imagination

Imagination, that is the key, you have to have imagination, or you'll never be free. Freedom is a state of mind, and you can have that all of the time. When you were just a little kid, your imagination took care of you with everything that you did, but as you grew older and started to learn, people started to dump on you with all of their concerns. They drove your imagination right out of your head and put negative thoughts in there instead.

Now is the time for us to relearn what we knew as a child before we started to learn. I've been there, I know what it's like to fly like an eagle through the night. People, let me tell you what I already know, you have to have imagination to let yourself go.

5-17-97
Immortal

I've had a good life, but I've had them before, each time I come back, I learn a little more. Life is an experience for each man, woman, or child, life is an experience that will last for just a little while. You can destroy the body, but you can't destroy the mind, the mind is energy, and it will last for all time.

Time is irrelevant, it doesn't mean a thing, it's your beliefs in life that time seems to bring. There's only one belief, one belief that you really need, and that's the belief in cosmic energy. It surrounds this planet and gives you everything that you need, it surrounds this planet with its life-giving energy.

When one door closes, another opens in your mind, and you're back again in some other lifetime, so it doesn't really matter when you die, because we'll all be back again for another try.

8-6-2000
In Control

My mind controls my body, but my body isn't really here, it's just an illusion I have had for forty-nine years. To experience the life, to experience the time, to experience the problems that are only "in my mind."

The body controls the outcome, but the outcome you choose, weather you Die, Win, or Lose. You experience the life that you chose to make all of your own, to experience evolution and see how you have grown.

This may sound a little weird, this may sound a little strange, but you experience life so the spirit will gain. We are all one, but most people will never believe, because they want to be in control of their own reality.

10-29-2000
Independent Thought

Domestication is for animals, so we've been told, but we have been domesticated since childhood in days of old. To think like our parents or what they call the norm, the independent thinker has never been born.

We are all like robots, the little tin man, we didn't have a brain, so how could we understand? We just followed the leader, which was Mom or Dad, and fell into the dream that the world had.

Independent thought, creativity too, is what the world needs now, and it's all up to you. You're not "STUPID," reality is just a dream, and dreams can be changed by just about any means. One independent thought, one creative idea too, could change this world for me and you.

6-3-03
Energetics

All things are connected and affected by one, the spirit, mind, and body, this energy belongs to everyone. Energetics, the mission of the mind to help all people realize their potential in a given amount of time.

To teach the public, to lend a helping hand , to incorporate this planet's energy whenever we can. The power of one is a nation on its own, the power of one with this energy we have sown.

10-24-95
Inner Man

I"ve been searching my whole lifetime for that inner man, searching my mind just to find out who I am.

I've done a lot of things when I was a kid just to find my niche in life, but I never did.

Someday, I'll find out just who I am, and then I'll know me and the inner man.

9-02-95
Insane

She gets out of work every night at two or three, then if she feels like it, she comes home to me. I'm getting tired of playing her games, playing her games is driving me insane.

You don't have much of a personality, it's true, but I'm in love, and there's nothing I can do. One day, I'll walk out, and I won't look back, I've just got to find a way to get on the right track.

9-2-97
Insight

The brain requires thought, thought requires time, intuition, on the other hand, comes straight from the mind. Look with your mind, not with your eyes, use your God-given ability we all have inside.

Think for yourself, not for your fellow man, and intuition will help you to understand. I have no desire to change this place, because it will evolve with the human race I have lived a million lifetimes on this planet of ours, but I have never found the real reason for who we are.

Insight will come to this planet of ours when we all learn to love just who we are.

5-10-97
Inspiration

I feel fine, yes, I do, I feel fine because I just found you. You're my inspiration for everything that I do, I'm so happy that I fell in love with you. I never felt like this before, you're all I need in life, and nothing more. Everything I do just seems to be oh-so-right, it's like walking out of the darkness and into the light.

Times will come when we don't always see eye-to-eye, but as long as we can remember this time, our love will never die. As we get older every day, the love we have will never fade away. You're my inspiration with everything I do, you're my inspiration, and I'm so in love with you.

4-21-97
Intuition

People do this every day, and it doesn't really matter what other people have to say. The paths of life are the paths you choose, let intuition and insight help to make the choices for you. Get out there in the field of dreams and let intuition and insight guide you, if you know what I mean.

Intuition is a feeling, insight is too, and they will help you find the better man that's inside of you. The energy is out there, and it's free for all of mankind, all you have to do is learn to use it to free your body and your mind.

8-30-96
Irrelevant

Time is the beginning, the beginning is the end, where man comes together, time begins. There is no time, time is only in your mind, if the world only knew what it will know in thirty years, time would all but disappear. The future, the past, the present, they are all the same, they are all happening now but on different plains.

I know this is a little hard to believe, but all you have to do is open your mind to see. That's the problem with the world of today, they all have blinders on, and they can only see one way. Your beliefs, they depend on time to fortify their existence in your mind.

7-17-04
It Can't Be Destroyed

I'm not sorry for the choices I choose, the decisions I make, or the things that I do. The same energy that takes me where I want to be is the exact same energy that I've lived with for all eternity. I create my own choices, I create whatever I do, I create with this energy, the energy that I use.

When I die, I know I will come back, quantum physics has already proven that. Energy, it just can't be destroyed, and it's the major part of every little girl and boy.

12-18-05
It Doesn't Seem Like Christmas

It doesn't seem like Christmas, although it's that time of year, it doesn't seem like the Holidays anymore around here. The days have grown shorter, the nights longer too, and I'm living this dream, but I'm living it without you. The memories of the season, the memories of the past keep filling my mind, and I'm happy at last.

Memories fade, the seasons do too, but I've just got to find a dream that doesn't include you.

10-11-96
It Don't Come Easy

It don't come easy when you're out on your own, the thoughts there just not there when you're all alone. You have to interact, look at the world in a different way, see things as they could be instead of as they are today.

Look at the colors of the sky, the colors of the trees, and the beauty that is there that they give to you and me. Some people call me a dreamer, but I'm not the only one, soon, we'll come together, and this world will be as one.

I don't know if I will see it or if it will be in my lifetime, but the world will come together for all of mankind.

By Jim Lozen

9-9-99
It's a Game Called Life

It's the game of life, and you play each hand, the choices are there for every man. Sometimes you win, and sometimes you lose, it all has to deal with the choices you choose. You have to know the colors and the token of each man to help you play this game, so you will better understand.

Colors are Auras, and Auras are the man, when you can see these colors, you will begin to understand. Intuition and intuitiveness will guide you too, it's a game called life that we all play even me and you.

9-29-02
It's All Up to You

It's weird how things happen, no matter what you say or do, it's weird how things happen, because the choice is still up to you. Choices are wrong, sometimes they're right, it all depends on what you created that night. Negative thinking, positive too, the choice is still yours, it's all up to you.

You created this planet, you created this time, you created everything that's happening in your own mind. You created your own problems, you created the outcomes too, you just didn't get there yet, but it's still all up to you. There are no problems, just answers for me and you, unless you create them, and it's all up to you.

4-5-97
Jeet Kune Do

You have to keep on moving, if you want to win this fight. You have to keep on moving right on through the night. Let your body take on over, let your muscles be relaxed, so you'll have the power and the intuition to act.

There's no such thing as weakness, just the inability to react, but if you keep on moving, you'll foil his attack. The energy from your opponent is all you need to win, and he's giving you that freely, so why not take advantage of him? With every movement he makes, the energy just flows, then all you have to do is wait for an opening, to deliver that decisive blow.

10-3-98
Jesus

December 25, 33 BC, there was a man born upon this World who changed it for all Eternity. He was a rebel that wanted change, and he wanted it all done in his father's name.

We created this Planet and all of the Treasure that it holds, with our minds and doing just as we were told. We created this evil that seems to thrive on its own by the hatred for our brothers that we have shown.

He showed us just how to live, he showed us by everything that he did. He showed us that with our minds, we can create, with every thought and breath that we take.

12-22-96
Jim

Long, long, long ago, there was a man named Jim who didn't seem to know. He didn't care how the world was meant to be, he could change it in his mind and make it the kind of world that he wanted it to be. He didn't talk much, he was kind of quiet and shy, but if you got to know him, he was quite a guy.

Astrology, he used to say, was the key, the mind is the door, and if you open it, you will begin to see. The Heavens above us and the tides down below are all part of what make the energy flow.

Energy is all you need, the energy of the mind, it will set you free. Through insight and inspiration, you'll know what's going to come, you'll be able to solve problems before they become one.

6-24-02
Just a Dream

This world is an illusion, just a book of dreams, and you can have anything, anything it seems. The mind is the power, the ego is the key, kill the ego and become one with me. Everything you think, do, or say has power within, because it's the energy of this day.

There is no time, there is no key, you have to realize this before you can see. The universe and all of its stars are just helpful little reminders of who we really are.

Number one answer, number one clue, the reality of this planet, it's you, baby, it's you.

11-25-2000
Just a Man

Believe what you want, for I am just a man and I can't explain what the world doesn't understand. We've been domesticated since childhood to follow a dream, the dream of this planet, its people, and all of their schemes. The colors of the rainbow are in every man, woman, and child, the colors of the rainbow that each of us can produce for just a little while.

The colors are always changing, every minute and hour of each day, positive and negative thinking seem to bring about the change in this way. I'm not here to teach you, "I don't really give a damn," but all you have to do is desire, and you will begin to understand. It may not be tomorrow, it may not even be next year, but all you have to do is desire, and your path will be made clear.

11-4-2000
Just an Illusion

I'm just an illusion in a world that doesn't exist, it's only in your mind, and you created all of this. This world as we know it is just a simple dream, a dream that goes on forever, as funny as that may seem.

We are all but energy, and energy can't be destroyed! We are all God's children, down to every last girl and boy. Energy can be altered, and energy can even be changed, but it can't be destroyed, and that's a proven fact in this little game.

Positive energy, that's all you need, it will make you or break you, but negative energy will take you right to your knees.

3-17-2000
Just Like Me

I was blinded by the light, but I could still see in this world of so-called reality. I finally realized everything was just energy, everything on this planet was just like me! Molecules and Neutrons as far as the eye could see, everything is an illusion, but it's still just energy.

You can't destroy it, so there is nothing that we can't do, all you have to do is think it, and it will come to you. An illusion that is in solid form is just an illusion that people have believed in, that's how it was born. Believe in yourself, that's all you have to do, and the energy of this planet will belong to you.

"Love is energy!" Love is all you need, love this planet and the Universe, we will all one day see.

1-20-96
Life

Life is a game that we all have to play, and it won't stop, it's here to stay. Times get tough every now and then, but before you know it, you're on track again.

Things will work out the way that they're meant to be, because it's all part of your destiny.

Some people think, life is like the wind, you go where it takes you, and you don't look back, but I don't agree with that, life is full of choices, and you've got to make the right ones, then life will be easy for everyone.

8-17-96
Killing Game

In the mist of battle when the war isn't won, there's always some guy out there who thinks he's just out there to have some fun. He'll take chances all the time, because he thinks he can't be killed, but little does he know that Charlie's waiting for him around the next hill.

A sniper gets him from above, and all hell breaks loose on the ground, people scatter everywhere to try to shoot old Charlie down.

Half of them are higher than kites, and the other half are space cadets, how can you win a war like this when all you want to do is forget?

9-30-99
Knowing

I am one with the planet, I am one with the trees, I am one with the Universe, because that is where I want to be. My desires are great, my desires are small, all I have to do is desire, and I can have anything at all.

The energy that surrounds this planet is the energy that I use, because the energy that surrounds this planet is simply just a tool. The clues are in the writings, and the writings are the word, the words have been taught for generations, so I know that everyone has heard.

He is the Oceans of this planet, he is the air that you breathe, he is everything around you, he is pure energy.

2-17-2000
Kristy with a "K"

You created me when you needed me, although I was here all of the time. I came into your life at your request, and I will be here until the end of time. Some people don't know this, some people don't care, but the time is "NOW!" There is no past, present, or future anywhere. You have always been here in some shape or form, and in the EONS to come, you are yet to be born.

In what you call the future or what you call the past, the spirit has always been here, it's the form that doesn't last.

5-13-96
Leaving

You have only been around for about a month or two. You say you're leaving now, but I'm in love with you.

I haven't known you long, there's no doubt about that, but what I have come to know, I'm in love with that. You're leaving my life for something better for you, I should be happy, but I'm not, and there's nothing I can do.

By Jim Lozen

3-21-96
Legacy

After I'm dead and gone, and my story comes to an end, my legacy will still go on, because my words will never end.

Death is the only adventure I've got to look forward to, because I've done everything on Earth that I have ever wanted to do.

Death bothers most people but not me, when my times up, it can have me. I'll start my new adventure with an open mind, because I'll be there for the rest of time.

9-2-96
Lessons

The moment is now, the power is here, we can make changes in our life, and our problems will seem to disappear.

What you think on a certain day becomes relative to your life in a certain way. Everything you think, everything you feel to your mind, it becomes real. Your thoughts have created the problems you are in, new thoughts can get you out, and you can start all over again. Your mind is your world, and you are the king, with it, you can have anything. I chose to write, that's what I do, and if I can change just one life, I have done what I came here to do.

We have all had many lives before, we just came back to learn a lesson that we hadn't learned before.

11-24-95
The Letter

I have done everything that I have ever wanted to do, done everything, but I have never gotten close to you, you're the only woman whom I have ever cared for, but for me, you wouldn't even open that door.

I wrote this letter just the other day, but it won't change things, and you'll never see things my way.

I wish I could change things and turn my life around, then I would be on top instead of down here on the ground.

Level

I've got a special time frame in my mind that I can go to to relax or unwind. When I'm at my level, there's no use in trying to bother me, because I'm somewhere else, and this is where I would rather be.

I'll go to the Mountains or down to the sea and visualize all of the beautiful scenery. This will clear my mind, and my journey has just begun, now it's time to delve into my past and have some fun. I can change things around, the way that they accrued, and set myself up for the kind of life that I deserve.

10-22-97
Liberate

Liberate your mind of the fears of all mankind, open up your heart with the compassion you had at the start. Life is but an illusion that has no end, I have lived a million lifetimes and will live them all again.

Blood on the highway, blood on the tracks, it doesn't really matter where it's at, the pain is still here, it doesn't go away until you liberate your mind of the fears you have today.

1-29-2000
Life Force

You come from the Heavens, you come from the Sea, you're all that I am, you're part of me! The energy from the Universe, the energy from the stars will take us on a journey and one day will teach us who we really are.

Time travels with the wink of an eye, a thousand years pass as another light-year goes by. You came to this planet with one goal in mind to accomplish your mission in one lifetime. Something goes wrong, something's amiss, you came back in the wrong period of time to accomplish this!

3-27-2000
Life Happens

Everything happens for a reason, everything happens in time, everything happens to a season, everything happens only in your mind. Life is like a garden that grows, life is like the winds that blow, life is like a cool summer's breeze, life is like all of these. Life is like a puzzle that you have to figure out, life is a game without a doubt.

The game of life that we have all been playing for all of these years is just that, so why should you show any signs of fear? You create with your mind, and then you choose, you create with your mind, so you have nothing to lose. The game of life is easy to play, but there are so many people who have nothing to say.

11-22-98
Lifetime

Don't bring me into your World, and I won't bring you into mine, we are but a vessel on a voyage of a lifetime. The oceans are deep, the rivers are blue, amnesia comes over each lifetime that I'm with you.

We have to remember what we did in the past to evolve in this lifetime, or we will repeat what we did last. We will do over and over the things that we have already done, and this World will grow stagnate, it won't evolve for anyone.

Themes of the future, reruns of the past, it's like a TV show, repeats always last.

4-15-01
Lifetimes

Domestication, or the way you were raised, will decide your fate one bright and sunny day. Time has no meaning, it's the theory of man to decide your fate, he figured he would lend you a helping hand. There is no remorse for anything that I ever did, because it was my choice in this land in which I live.

Different cultures, different times, different beliefs set in the mind. You choose your own life, you choose your own parents too, you choose everything that you desire to do. Life is an illusion, God's gift to man, to experience life in ways that he still doesn't understand. The energy that surrounds us is the reality of our dreams, and we imagine this world, "or as it should seem."

2-09-95
Lost Love

Girl, I love you more each and every day, but I can't tell you, because I wouldn't know what to say. I tell myself tomorrow, but tomorrow never comes, I'm scared of being rejected, but then I tell myself this could be the one.

I'll probably never tell you, because that's the way I am, I've been that way all my life I hope you'll understand.

I keep trying to forget you, but every time I try, something always happens and makes me want to cry. I know you'll never see me the way that I see you, can't get you out of my mind, and I don't know what to do.

8-23-98
Life's Destiny

We are just thoughts, illusions of the mind, we are just energy that will last for many lifetimes. Energy surrounds this planet, energy upholds and binds, with this energy, we created this planet, and our destiny is yours and mine.

We create whatever happens, it's our choice, no matter what we do, there is no evilness about us, there is no devil down below, just the choices we take, the destiny we make, and the life that we put it through.

7-22-2000
Life's Energy

We are all energy, spirits of the mind, we are all one in this human race that we call mankind. Everything that happens, everything that we do affects someone else in this life that we happen to choose. If we choose to be a teacher, a lawyer, or such, we would affect the lives of the people we touch.

I chose my life, I even chose my destiny, I chose all of this before I was created so this would be an easier life for me. Life's choices, they are all of your own, the funny part about this is you choose them before you are born. You chose your own life, you even made a plan, all you have to do now is remember, so you will better understand.

8-12-2000
Life's Quest

Mistakes in life that came your way aren't really mistakes, they are blessings that came that day. They may be a little hard to figure out in your mind, but trust me, they will all benefit you given enough time.

The world, it's just an illusion that you create as you go, and you manifest all of your desires with the energy that flows. Your mistakes are your desires at this point in time, and they will fulfill all of your reality in your present state of mind. The Quest for Life and no one is in control, all you have to do is desire as your life unfolds.

1-12-02
Light Is Love

I create with my mind, or is this all a dream, we created this World, or so it would seem. Light is the answer, light is the key, light is our one and only destiny.

We are reality, we create it every day by the things that we see or the things that we say. Light is energy, and energy can't be destroyed, light is the building blocks of every girl and boy.

Money doesn't matter when you can create whatever it is that you need by the light from the sun and this thing that we call energy.

8-19-03
Lights Out

August 14, 2003, Michigan went dark, and so did we. Detroit City, Roseville too, East Point was without power, and there wasn't anything that we could do. The police were out walking their beats and directing traffic in the streets. Cell phones were out, cordless too, the old plug-in was the only thing that we could use.

When daylight fades and darkness sets in, the crooks come out, but it just didn't begin. The times, they are changing for every man, now we help our brothers whenever we can. The power was gone for just three days, but still, it affected so many lives in so many ways.

7-28-98
Liquid Courage

This is liquid courage that I hold in my hand, and if I drink it down, I'm not afraid of any man. I'm always sitting here, almost every night drinking this stuff, so I'm ready to fight, now one of these days, I'll get out of here, but if I do that, where will I get my beer?

Saturday night is my favorite night of all, because I can drink all night until I get ready to fall. Sunday morning, I can just lie in bed or live over the toilet and wish I was dead.

1-4-97
Little Girl

Go away, little girl, I don't need you anymore. I know what you're like, and you won't get through my door. Things are different than they were way back when, and I don't need you to call a friend.

Times change over the years, and I don't need you as a friend, and I don't want you around here. You messed up my life once before, and you won't get the chance to do it anymore. Trust is what life is all about, you have to trust in someone, then love will come about.

Love is such a beautiful thing, but if you don't trust in the one you love, think of all the trouble it can bring.

9-7-97
Lives

Lives that I have created, lives that I have lived, it doesn't really matter what I was or what I did. I was sent here to experience life, to experience life in every way, and then when my mission was completed, I had no other reason to stay.

I chose everything that I wanted to do, I chose to be with people like you, to enlighten each other, to do the best we can, to enlighten each other so we would understand. Understanding each other and learning to love is why we were sent here from the heavens above.

8-10-95
Lonely People

The times, they are changing, this world is coming to an end, sometimes it looks pretty hopeless, living life without a friend. the days, they are lonely, people keep putting you down, life isn't worth living when there's nobody around, but then something happens to turn things all around, and it really doesn't matter that nobody's ever in town .

9-1-01
Look at Me

Hey, girl, look at me, look in to my eyes and tell me what you see. The colors of the ocean, the colors sea, the colors of the rainbow, they are all inside of me. The colors change from day to day, it all depends upon my mood or what I have to say. When I get angry or when I get mad, the colors change abruptly from what I had.

I live in the "Now," the present time, when nothing can happen unless it enters the mind. This world is an illusion, and we are too, the colors are energy, and that's all we will ever need to use.

2-26-96
The Lost Continent

In the Antarctic under thousands of tons of ice and snow, stood an Island known as Atlantis, which flourished many years ago.

This Island was populated by an advanced civilization, or so the story is told, a race of super humans that died out long ago.

The Earth shifted on its axis, which it does from time to time. It killed off the Dinosaurs and all of mankind. The Continents moved, and Atlantis was one of them. It ended up as Antarctica, and its people were never heard from again.

By Jim Lozen

2-17-02
Love Is All Around

Love is all around us, love is in everything, the beauty of a forest, the power of a stream. We are light, and that's all we are, light from the Heavens and light from the stars. The energy that's in each and every one is the exact same energy directed from the sun.

Molecules and neutrons, that's all we will ever be, the molecules and neutrons that make up this energy. We are one, it doesn't matter who you are, we are all one with this energy from the stars. The past has gone, it's already been destroyed, the future is now, and it's in every girl and boy.

2-23-2000
Love Is All You Need

What we learn is from the Ego, but what we need is from the Heart. The Ego teaches knowledge and fear, and without that, you're doomed from the very start. The Heart teaches love for your brothers and your sisters, love for this whole land, and without this love for the planet, we are also doomed, but many people just don't seem to understand.

The Ego is like a drug that you don't really need, because the Ego just seems to get in the way of all of your possibilities. All you need is Love for this planet and Love for yourself, God will do the rest for you and everyone else.

2-10-02
Love Is Energy

I am the light, I am the day, I am the illusion of each person I play. Death doesn't matter, the dream still goes on, it's just part of this journey and part of this song. This song is love, energy is too, this song is life for me and you.

This world is easy, it's but a dream, you create all of your desires so everything is as it should seem. Learn from the Masters or learn on your own, learn from this energy that you have sown.

The moment is now, the past has already been destroyed, learn from this new energy that's in every girl and boy. Don't expect anything, just know it will be, because this is the way of total energy. A gift from the heavens, a gift from above, total energy is nothing but love.

4-7-02
Love Is Forever

We die every moment of each and every day, we die every moment as the time just seems to fade away. Each hour, minute, second too, after all none of these energy's belong to me or you. It's ours for the asking, we create every day, we create this illusion of life and the games people play. If only for one second, you could see who you really are, the shadow of darkness would be lifted, and we could reach for every star.

The process would be over, love would fill the land, the energy of this universe would enter into each and every man. The power of the universe is yours to command, the power of the light is ours, if we could only understand.

4-2-2000
Love Is the Answer

Love is the answer, love is the "Key," love is the destination of humanity. I don't know when we'll get there, but it can't be long, because love is the answer for a world gone wrong. We are but one, just you and me, we are all part of our ever changing reality. Reality changes from day to day, with every thought and word that you say. Saying is one thing, meaning is too, if you mean what you say, this world would be a better place for me and you.

Love is the answer, and we can start today, love is the answer, and the light will show us the way.

5-30-2000
Love Is the Secret

Every little syllable, every word I say is brought about as words of love as I pass this way. The Solar winds and breeze affect the things I do, but whatever I am capable of, I do it all through you.

You're my inspiration, you're everything that I see, you're the World around us, you're also part of me.

My mission is simple as one, two, three to bring love to this Planet for all Eternity. Love is the secret, love is the key, love is our "DESTINATION" in a World that we cannot see.

6-14-95
Memory

Towns by towns that I travel through, I've just got to keep looking, because I'm looking for you.

You're just a memory from a long time ago, but I can see you oh-so-clearly wherever I go.

I'll keep looking in every town I go with the hopes of finding you because I just can't let you go.

5-11-02
Mama's Day

As long as I have you to guide the way, my life has meaning to it every single day. You taught me the lessons and how to make dreams come true, you taught me I could have everything, because you are me and I am you. What I do for others, I do for me, we are all one in this reality.

The energy that guides us, the energy that binds is the energy of this planet, and it's yours and mine. I love you, Mama, what more can I say than I love you, Mama, every single day?

9-13-97
Magic

The magic that is here, it was put here for you, it's called energy, and it's something we all can use. You can find this in the flowers and the trees and other people, they will even give you their energy.

You don't have to fight for it, there's plenty of room, it comes with each morning, sunset, and bloom. Man thought it was his and his all alone, which created corruption in times unknown. The energy is out there, there's enough for everyone, there's enough for every creature under the sun.

2-16-2000
Mama

My mama done told me when I was a boy that I'm here for a reason, not to play with my toys. She told me the mind, that is the key, develop the mind, and the world would be an easier place for me.

Everything around you is just an Illusion of the mind that you have created and create all of the time. The people around you, you create as you need for inspiration and to fulfill all of your needs. I'm a lot older than I was way back then, when I was given this advice from my best friend.

9-7-96
Man

The past is your future, your future is your past, what goes around comes around, time will never last. The need for power has corrupted everyone, but power is abundant, there's enough for anyone.

The energy that flows is the only power that you need, and you can get that from the flowers and the trees, the sea and the ocean are another source you can use, with it, you'll have all the power anyone can ever use.

The power inside is the power of the man, God didn't make no junk, and it's time the world understands. Anything that happens, anything that's now, you create in your mind anyhow.

11-29-96
Manuscript

You have to join the four elements to become alive, you have to join the four elements to come up with five. The fifth is Ether, which is pure energy, everything has it, even the flowers and the trees.

The Druids knew this, they came up with all five, but the Church didn't like their teachings, so they had to hide, if you've read *The Tenth Insight*, you know just what they did, they took the Manuscript with them, and then they hid. They went underground with their teachings, because they had to hide, they went underground with their teachings to keep them alive. The Church didn't like their teachings, because they would lose control, and power corrupts, everybody knows.

3-18-2000
Marriage

To the married couple, life is going to change! It's not just you anymore, there's someone else in the game. Life is like a roller coaster, there's a lot of ups and downs, just learn to hang on tight when those tough times come around.

Each one of us are different, no one is quite the same, but just remember that love is the answer, it's the whole nine innings of the game.

Love the "Old Lady" and "Love the Old Man" and Love the "Kids," even if they don't understand. Love is the answer, "Love is all you Need," Love gives the Earth its life-giving energy.

2-15-97
Martial Arts

My life was at a standstill, the years were just passing me by, then I got this letter from this weird little guy. He said come on over and give martial arts a try, it will open a few doors for you that you haven't even tried. I thought about it for a while before I decided to go, but let me tell you when I went the energy just began to flow.

Energy is something that isn't that easy to find, but it's out there, and all you have to do is open up your mind. I started writing again, something I haven't done for twenty some years, this time, the doors were open, the people they all wanted to hear.

I've made the hall of fame in the poetry arts, I've also got five songs out there, and I owe it all to the martial arts.

6-25-2000
Master Key

The Mayans, the Incas, and the Aztecs too have already done what we are just beginning to do! Use the mind for all of mankind to barter and trade instead of using the money we made. The mind is like a window that we open at night, in the morning, it lets in all of the light. The light is the universe, the power of the air, the energy mixes in, and we are there.

What goes around comes around, and it is our time, the secrets of the universe belong to all of mankind. In the valley far below under just about a quarter inch of snow lies the key that you have been looking for, the key to the universe and all of the doors. Locked or open, somehow you will know that other people have been here long ago.

9-19-97
Master

Nothing lasts forever, everything comes to an end, there is no permanence about us, the road is long but has no end. With each life that we live here, we have to learn again, memories die hard with dreams that never end.

The Master's words are with us, they're written on the wind, with each breeze that goes by now, the Master comes again. The creator of this planet, the creator of the stars, created the Universe, and he created who we are.

By Jim Lozen

Meditation

Help me, "G," I love you, man , if you can't do this, no one can. Help me, "G," I know that my body is dormant, I know that it will never age, it will never get sick, and it will never die until I choose or I decide. Help me "G," I know that all of my desires will come true the instant I think of them, because they all come through you. I know that I can see auras any time of the day, all I have to do is focus, and the auras, they come my way.

Thank you, "G," for all of the teachers I've had during this life, thank you for giving me the ability to understand them, and thank you for being there when I didn't understand them, you were always there to lead me down the right road. Thank you, "G," I love you, man, if you can't do this, no one can.

2-1-04
Memory's Forever

Long as I remember, you'll always be right here, the energy that you possessed will never disappear. I think about you daily, you're always on my mind, and in the evening when I sleep, we're together all the time. Memory's forever, we create them every way, memory's forever until our dying day.

Creation is our right, our power, and our need, with this energy that we possess, we create everything that we see. Choices and decisions, it's all up to you, we create anything and everything that we can really use.

6-16-01
Memories of the Past

I don't worry, worry is brought about by time, and time doesn't exist, you create that with in your own mind. We live in the now, the present time where nothing can go wrong unless it enters the mind. Age doesn't happen without time, and sickness doesn't exist unless it enters the mind.

The mind is the enemy, we're under his thumb, and there's no way out for anyone. Take the backseat, sit in the chair , because as long as he rules, we're not going anywhere. Memories of the past, in the future, times are just memories he uses to enforce this thing that we call time.

Live with no mind, because that is the way to be, live with no mind, and this world will open up, and you will begin to see. I am Immortal, time has no meaning for me, I live in the now, because that's where I desire to be.

7-7-96
Message

If I could convey a message with each word that I write down, the message would be to love one another, because you won't always be around.

The days, they pass so quickly, and you can't turn back the hands of time, everything that has happened, you just put away in the back of your mind. The good times and the bad, they're all in there for you, when judgment day comes, you'll know then what you didn't do.

Chances keep coming to right the wrong that you did, but if you don't have an open mind, you'll just keep repeating the same things that you did.

7-3-2000
Meteor

The black rains fell all through the night, and the North winds blew until the morning light. The vegetation was just beginning to grow, and the people of the Earth, they just seemed to know that change was about to come and it would affect everyone. The change we had been waiting for for twenty some years, the change, in a moment, it would appear.

Twenty-six years ago on this date in time, a Meteor struck this planet and changed the course of history for all of mankind. The Earth exploded in one big blast, and the soot that covered it came from out of the past. We took to living underground, because that was the only safe place that could still be found.

This was the new beginning for all of mankind, he could build the Utopia he has only dreamt about for an entire lifetime.

3-8-97
Millennium

When people come together, we will finally begin to learn that the physical body is of no real concern. We will learn Telepathy and be able to enter each other's mind and go forward or backward in the space of time.

Through insight and inspiration and soul groups of all kind, we will deal with each problem of the planet as it comes to mind. The Ozone layer is depleting, but through focused energy from the mind, we were able to put it back until the end of time. The job will be completed in about twelve years, then life will last another Millennium or until it disappears.

Focus on your problems, and insight will help you too, it will bring out the better man that's inside of you.

10-14-01
Mind, Memory, and You

I've got all of the words for the next poem in my mind, I've just got to put them all together to make them rhyme. Life is an illusion, but then again your dreams are too, and they are also a part of you. The Bible says it, and I quote, "Father, Son, and Holy Ghost," for your interpretation, pick the words that you choose, "Mind, Memory, and Me or You."

We are all one, I know that's kind of hard to believe, but we are all one in this same reality. We create who we are, we create what we say, and we will always do this creating each and every day.

There is no secret about this, we don't even need any clues, because we have everything that we will ever need or use.

Mind and Soul

The mind and the spirit, two separate entities, both living in one's body, both trying to be set free. The mind wants to experience things that he has learned while the spirit all he wants is to return. Two separate entities pulling in different ways, two separate entities each and every day.

Teach your kids the knowledge that they need to grow, but teach your kids the knowledge that will let the energy flow. Energy and insight, they go hand in hand, and together, they will turn this country into a better land.

Learn by the experience of just a few, learn by the experience of what not to do. History is a misprint, it just shows one point of view, it will never show you what the other side was really trying to do.

2-5-2000
Mind Control

Meditation is a form of prayer, meditation will guide your life and take you just about anywhere. Through insight and intuition, it will guide you to options you never thought you had or could use.

Life is easy with mediation at your side, because everything that you need will just come inside. All of your dreams and desires are waiting right by the door, all you have to do is open it, because there is so much more. This world is filled with possibilities that we can find to better this planet for all of mankind.

4-18-95
Mind's Eye

I've got thoughts running through my mind, I can't help it if they all rhyme.

I used to write songs for a rock band I was in, when the band finally quit, I never wrote again.

I started writing just four months ago, and it will take me anywhere I want to go.

You can be anywhere you want to be, just develop your mind, and it will set you free.

8-16-96

As I look out across this valley and watch the sun come up like it has since the beginning of time, it transports me to some other place in the far reaches of my mind.

I'm all alone in this world of mine, and there's no place to go, all the memories just come flooding in from so many years ago. They seem so real at the time that I'll just relive them in the back of my mind. Things I haven't thought of for so many years just come to the front as they reappear.

I have to live them over just one more time, because I'm stuck here in the back of my mind.

2-24-2000
Miracle

You don't have to believe this, not many people do, but you don't have to read *A Course in Miracles*, because the Miracle is you. You are one with the father, one with the son, and one with the holy spirit, because the love has already begun.

Try as you might, try as you will, the Creator never made a mistake, and he never will. We were put here to create all of the time, anything at will, with the help of the mind. The body is but a tool that we use to get around, but the spirit and the mind is what we take when we go to town. There's no way around this, there's nothing that you can't do, so you might as well join the rest of us and become part of the holy spirit too.

By Jim Lozen

5-02-95
Missing You

I'm missing you already, and you haven't even gone. All the dreams that could have been have suddenly gone wrong.

There's nothing I can say or do to keep you here with me, so I'll just say have a good life and please remember me.

10-10-98
Mistakes

Mistakes that I have made, I have made quite a few, living life the way that I do. The actions that have passed through my mind are the places that I have been to throughout my entire lifetime.

If I could forget and leave these places behind, there might be a different man within my mind, but these places are part of me, if I forget them, I forget the real me. I needed these places to make the man, to complete the Mission and take my stand.

12-12-98
Mistress

I don't want to know your secrets, I don't want to know your age, I don't want to know anything about you, because it would spoil the FANTASIES that we play. I created you with all my wants and all my needs, I created you the way I wanted you to be.

You're here at this moment, you're here at this time, you're here for me, girl, if only in my mind. We CREATE what we want, we CREATE what we need, we CREATE with our minds, because it's all part of a human's DESTINY.

7-26-98
Molecules and Neutrons

I know that one day this will happen, I know that one day you will be mine. I believe in the universal consciousness and the power of the mind. The energy that surrounds this planet, the energy that upholds and binds is the energy that will always be there until the end of time.

Molecules and Neutrons, things the naked eye can't see, everything on this planet has its own special kind of energy. Liquid energy, energy in a can, the power is there, but man still doesn't understand.

6-15-01
Moment

Now is forever, there is no time, time is a domestication that has been put in our minds. We only learn what we are taught through the eons of yesterdays, which are not. Yesterday never happened, tomorrow will never come, the time is now, always for everyone. Yesterday is tomorrow, tomorrow is today, they're just words that mean nothing, because the time is today.

The future is the present, the present is our past, what we do now we've done before, this moment will always last. Time means nothing, and our story has no end, what we do now we repeat over and over and over again.

Now is forever, and we all have survived, this moment of enlightenment has made "this body come alive."

9-7-96
Moments in Time

The past is gone, it's just a memory in your mind, and you can't go back again, it's lost for all time. It's just a moment that passed, and it isn't anymore, you just passed through that open door. Pathways and doors, you have nothing to lose, because you can't go back again once you choose.

Time waits for no man, so you'd better choose fast, because if you don't, it'll be in the past.

1-25-97
Money

Love me like you do, like you did last night, love me like you did when you held me so tight. I didn't see it coming, I didn't know what was wrong, but you came into my life with a love that was so strong. I don't know what tomorrow will bring, but with you by my side, tomorrow doesn't mean a thing.

Love me like you do, like you did last night, love me like you did when you held me oh-so-tight. I want to live with you, baby, I want to make you mine, I want to stay here for you, baby, until the end of time. Money can buy just about anything, but money can't buy you love, and without love, life doesn't mean a thing.

8-13-2000
Mood Ring

This world is but an illusion that you have created within a dream, this is our reality, but it isn't quite what it seems. All of your desires, your wants, and needs are created through yourself with the help of energy.

The energy that surrounds this planet is simply just a tool, so the energy that surrounds this planet is the energy that we use. The mind controls the body, but the body really isn't here, it's just a simple tool that we have created throughout thousands of years.

We are but pure energy, and we have our color too, the colors, they vary with the choices we choose. Reds, greens, yellows, and blues, it all depends on the change in your mood.

10-19-2000
Mountaintop

Sitting on a mountaintop, breathing in fresh air, the winds are gently blowing, rustling through my hair. The colors, they are changing, changing rapidly in my mind, the colors of the rainbow, which are so very hard to find.

One day, I'll reach enlightenment, one day, I will find that this planet coexists with the body and the mind. One can't live without the other, one lives for just a day, one works constantly, they coexist in this way.

This planet was created by you and you alone, with your desires and your needs, your reality was shown.

3-13-95
Muk Yum

Something happened just the other night, blew my mind, it was out of sight. I went to my level like I always do, when the trailer started rocking, my mind was coming unglued.

I kept telling myself, I would be all right, that this would pass with the night, I saw a lot of things running through my mind, and they will all come to pass with the passage of time. Don't ask me how I know all of this, because I won't say, I doubt that you would believe me anyway.

4-12-98
Multiple Personalities

Multiple personalities, I've got three, there's the roofer, the writer, and then there's me. Each one of these will change me, it depends on the time of day which one I become and which one goes away. The writer, he'll show up just about any time of day, it all depends what's going on and what I have to say.

The roofer, he'll show up at 7:30 until 3:00, he's the logical one that's inside of me, and then there's Jim, he's the one who's all messed up inside, doesn't really care, just goes along for the ride, he's like a little kid that's inside of me, he has all the knowledge and know-how but doesn't really care what the world may see.

11-6-96
Out of My League

You're out of my league, I don't have much of a chance without your love, darling, but you won't even give me a glance.

Something must have happened in some other space and time, something must have happened in some other lifetime.

Time passes so quickly from one life to the next, it's like a merry-go-round, but we never seem to forget. Everything that happens, everything that's on our minds just seems to travel with us through each of our lifetimes. You're out of my league, and I don't know what to do, you're out of my league, but I'm still in love with you.

2-21-97
Nature

When winter sets in, nature falls asleep to rejuvenate the energy our bodies just can't seem to keep. The colors have changed, but the power's still there, the energy can still be found most anywhere.

Open your mind, the power is within, every man has the power he needs as the day begins. The snow on the porch, the snow in the streets is the only color you have to work with, so you have to cheat.

Imagine a world filled with different colors and hues, imagine a world filled with all the energy that you can ever use. This is where meditation can help you too, it can give you all the power and energy that you need to use.

Winter is the dead time of the year when nature falls asleep and peace is here.

4-26-98
New Beginning

He was a horse thief in Canada back in 1893, his name was Arthur Lauzon, and it turns out he's related to me. He was deported, and he came over here. Immigration spelled his name wrong, and the Lauzon family seems to have disappeared.

He had a second chance in life, a new beginning if you will, to start all over again and try to make it to the top of the hill. New beginnings are what we all need every now and then, new beginnings so we can start all over again.

2-28-96
Nightmare

When your tour of duty is over and you finally come home again, you think you're going to be all right, but that's when the nightmares begin. I try not to think about it much, but every night I'm back again in the rice paddies of Vietnam, where I lost some of my best friends.

Someday, I hope these dreams will be over, but I must have left something behind, because I just keep reliving one time frame in my mind.

6-10-01
No Mind

I live in the now, the present time where nothing can happen unless it enters the mind. There is no past or future time, there is only the present as it unwinds. The past and the future, this thing that we call time, it's our reality, but it's only in the mind. We create everything that we do, but we're lost without time, so that's what we use.

Imagine a world where there is no time, no disease, because it has to enter the mind. We create everything that we do, but without time, we would have nothing to use. No aging of the body without time, no corruption of this planet, because it's only in the mind.

8-4-02
Nothing Is Evil

Nothing is evil unless you make it that way, nothing is evil unless you create it today. Creating is thinking, thinking is time, and we created everything within one's own mind. You created the mountains, you created the seas, you created the oceans, and you even created me.

Energy is all this world is made of, the energy of this planet is nothing but love. Different shapes, different forms, it has been your choice since the day you were born. This world is eternal, and so are we, because this energy I speak of is you and me. You can't destroy us, energy is for all time, the body we live in is just a state of mind.

12-1-98
NOW

The Past, the Present, the Future, it's all happening at this point in time, but people can't comprehend this, because it's a matter for the Mind. I know I have written this, I have written this before, all I have to do is remember the words, and I'll write it once more.

I'm in the Future, I'm also in the Past, the PRESENT isn't Relative, because it doesn't seem to LAST. Remembering, that's what we all have got to learn to do, because in remembering the Past, the Future will just seem so right for everything that you do.

If we could all remember at one certain point in time, this would seem like Heaven on Earth, and it wouldn't have to be in just one MAN'S mind.

3-31-2000
Nurture

It is your beliefs in life that will cut you down, and it is your beliefs in life that makes the world go around. If you live negatively all of the time, the world will accommodate you, if only in your mind. If you live positively, the world will nurture you and help you out with whatever you decide to do.

I write, that's what I do, and if I can help just one person, then I have done what I came here to do. Believe in yourself, and there's nothing that you can't do, believe in yourself, and this world belongs to me and you.

Old beliefs are useless if they don't help you anymore, make new beliefs that will nurture you in a way that you never knew before. Become one with this planet in whatever you do, and the energy of this planet will guide and protect in you.

10-29-2000
October 31st

As the shadows of darkness fall over this land, the Goblins and Witches will make their stand. Blood running down the walls outside, and the Headless Horseman will take his bride.

This is the only time of year when strange things happen and people disappear. "Wanda Leadbetter" was her name, and she said, "This was all foolishness," and she wasn't going to play our "SCARY" little game!

Nobody knows where Wanda resides today, because the Headless Horseman just took his bride and rode away.

3-28-2000
Older by Choice

Back in my younger days when life was fun, I was filled with energy and loving just about everyone! Those days have gone, they just slipped away, and now I just seem to be getting older each and every day.

Older by choice, that isn't really who I am, so I think I'll just change my mind and be the best that I can. Time may pass, but I will never fade away, and I'm making that choice here and now today. Life is filled with choices, it's part of the game, and if you make the right choices, your life will never be the same. Choose the wrong path, and life will go down, but choose the right one, and fame and fortune will be found.

1-31-97
Older

The days are over when I was young and life was filled with so much fun. Them days are gone, they're just a thing of the past, and I'll never have a chance again to do what I did last.

The times, they are changing, they're changing awful fast, and all I have are memories to protect the past. Memories, some are good, and some are bad, and some I wish I never had. I had a friend, I can't even remember his name, he died a long time ago, but now it seems like it's all in vain.

Memories are something you never want to lose, they make you who you are, and they're something that you can't choose.

12-21-03
Once upon a Time

Once upon a time in a land not so far away, the future was born, and it has created this very day. The time was now, the future was already here, and man finally realized what he couldn't make disappear.

The energy of this planet, the energy of the stars, the energy of this universe defines just who we really are. You can't destroy it, and you can't control what you cannot see, the energy of this planet is you and me. We are all born with this power of eternal light, born with this power to create day from night. Positive energy is all you need, negative distinguishes what you cannot see.

5-26-01
ONE

The now is the future from the past that we have lived in before but refused to grasp. The future is ours, the past is too, all you have to do is remember, and this world belongs to you.

Problems are irrelevant, problems don't even exist, problems are something that you have created out of all of this. Thought is creation, thought is the mind, and it never stops working, it's working all of the time. The energy that's inside of the birds and the bees is the exact same energy that's inside of me. We are all one, it's plain to see that we are this world's destiny.

We have created disease, destruction, pestilence too, but when are we going to create something we can really use.

6-15-95
Orders

A thunderous silence came from the valley below, we were all scared, but we knew that's where we were going to go.

Tommy, Johnny, Billy, and me, we were on a search-and-destroy mission to set some people free. We did this every now and then, because we were the best way back when.

People don't know what we went through, killing these people was a hard thing to do, but we had orders from old Uncle Sam, win by attrition, kill anything that moved down to the very last man, if we got caught, we were on our own, because Uncle Sam would deny us and say we did it alone.

5-30-99
Our World

Reality is a dream, a dream of the mind that will take you on a journey throughout your entire lifetime. Dreams are an interpretation of things that you think you see, and with dreams, this becomes part of your reality.

Reality is a focal point for things that are meant to be, but if it's only a dream, you can change your reality. I just want to make a suggestion, I just want to give you a clue, you can change anything, because it's all just part of being you.

The Earth, the trees, the sky up above, we are all but Energy and filled with nothing but love.

By Jim Lozen

11-19-01
Our Time

I live in the "Now," the present time, I live in this moment because it's all mine. The future is ours, so is the past, but the moment is "Now," and it will always last. Time is the Ego, Ego is time, domestication is this planet and all of its kind. We only know what we have learned, and in the generations before us, we all took our turn.

What goes around comes around, it's always the same, we all took our turn, and we all played this same game. I live in the moment, which will always be mine, I live in the "Now," because this is "OUR TIME."

3-3-2000
Outcome of the Mind

I'm wide awake, but this is only in my dreams, while my body is resting, it sets my soul free. I wander this planet, the fear is gone, without an ego, nothing can go wrong.

I can go anywhere with just a thought, do anything that I desire or want. Rules were just made to be broken, rules are just beliefs that you have had implanted in your mind, rules that were created by the whole of mankind.

Make new beliefs, beliefs that you can use, and these new beliefs will become part of you.

1-6-2000
Outcome

Problems aren't problems, they are choices that you made so you could have the experience you are having today. Go down the right path, and your problems, they fade away just like the energy of each night and day.

Just like the dreams that you have every night, problems are there to help you turn on the eternal light. Grow with your problems as you grew once before, and the Universal conciseness and the eternal light will meet at the door.

9-19-04
Power of Enlightenment

You can kill the body, but you can't destroy me, for I am one with this universe, I am total energy. I am one with the oceans, one with the trees, one with the flowers, the birds, and the bees. We all find enlightenment whenever we can, the universe takes control when we are ready to understand.

The oceans, the rivers, the mountains, and the streams, these are all different forms of energy, all we have to do is understand that we are all one with this universe, this energy that we call man.

10-29-96
Pages

In the school of life, there are always lessons to be learned, and with it, the pages of your mind will be turned. Your mind is like an open book with pages to be filled, your memory is the pen you use, or is it called a quill?

Each year that passes is a page, and your memory jots it down, whenever you have to remember something, your mind will always bring it around. When you go through life, your story unfolds, there is always something to be learned or a story to be told.

There's always a reason, and there's always a plan God cerates in every man.

7-12-95
Pain

I've never liked making new friends, because I knew I would have to leave them in the end.

It hurts every time I have to say good-bye, but the pain hurts so bad, I wish I would die.

I've lived like a hermit most of my life, because I don't know when the pain will hit me, it comes and goes, it's something I have to learn to live with, we all have our crosses to bear, this is mine, and I'm living in despair. I'll have my good days and my bad, there's not really too much I can do except muddle through life doing the best that I can do.

Paralyzed

I woke up in Virginia on this cold and raining day, the last thing I remember, I was in Vietnam, and it was a Tuesday, it's kind of scary where I am, I've got all these tubes inside me, and I don't understand. Something must have happened, something must have went wrong, because the last thing I remember, I was on a search-and-destroy mission in Vietnam.

I've got all these little tubes running in and out of me, I'm paralyzed on the left side, and I can't see. I wish I would have died there on that little piece of land, that little piece of land back in Vietnam.

3-10-98
Passage of Time

Time passes so quickly, or is it just a thought that's running through my mind, or could this be a dream that I am having at this point in time?

My eyes are wide open, and now I can see that the mind is the source of pure energy, anything that happens, it's happening at this point in time, there is no past or future, just the energy of the mind.

I wish I could tell you, but you wouldn't believe that time is also the source of pure energy.

3-20-98
Past Life Regression

We were born the same, just you and me, but we were born in different centuries. I was you, and you were me, past life regression has helped me to see. Time is like a river that will always flow, energy can't be stopped and evolution will always grow.

The life I live now for a very short time is the life I chose for this mission of mine. This mission will reveal itself in time, but as for now, it's buried deep within my mind.

11-4-99
Past, Present, Future

We are all but Energy, Illusions of the mind, Atoms and Neutrons, evolution at a certain point in time. What you desire you create with your mind, it all has to deal with the now that we call time. Time is a big factor, but it really shouldn't be, because the time is now and will be for all eternity.

Whatever you do, whatever you say, you do it in the now that is today. The past, the future aren't quite what they seem, because now is the future of all your dreams.

7-03-95
Peace

To pray for peace, it's a just cause, but it's not going to work, that's a lost cause. Today it's the me generation living around here, what have you done for me lately is all you hear. We've got to stick together if we want to get anything done, and you know that's not going to work, because you can't count on anyone. To pray for peace, that is a just cause, but to pray for peace, that's like believing in Santa Claus.

1-28-01
Pebbles

Take me as I am or as I choose to be, for this is my very own chosen reality. I chose my own life, I chose my own way, and I'll be like this until my dying day. I'm responsible for my actions, I'm responsible for everything that I do, there is no one to blame, not him or you.

Life is like a pebble that you drop into a spring, the ripples continue endlessly until they engulf everything. You create your own problems, you create your solutions too, with an open mind, everything will come to you.

Different shapes, different forms on this planet, the energy was born. You can't destroy it, it's always on the move, and the funny part about it is this energy was created as me and you!

2-26-2000
People

The energy that is within an object is the exact same kind of energy that is part of you, the molecules are different, but the energy is the same, the energy is you. People say we're different, but we're not, we're really quite the same, the energy that surrounds this planet is the only energy in the game.

Life is but an illusion that you can change at any given time, because life is but an illusion, an illusion of the mind. You say you don't know how to do this, you say you don't even want to play, well, I've got news for you, baby, you play this game every day.

9-24-96
Perception

The door to perception is hidden deep within your mind, but you can break on through that door at any given time. This door to enlightenment on the other side is a hard door to break through, but it's worth it if you try.

The problems that you have, the answers you will receive, it's just like being one with all of Earth's entities. I've been there before, I've passed through that door to the other side where life is so alive.

The people who are there are not like you and me, they're just a ball of light, nothing but pure energy. They speak with their minds, they don't even say the spoken word, but there's so much you can learn from them, and to think, they don't even say a word.

1-8-97
Pitfalls

The minutes keep passing, time keeps moving on, life is passing you by, and pretty soon, it will be gone. The weeks, they turn into months, the months turn into years, and before you know it, it's your turn to disappear. The road ahead is rocky, there's an easier one on the right, but you know deep down in your heart that you must travel forward tonight.

Life is full of pitfalls that you must overcome, and you know by doing your best, these pitfalls, you will have won. Time waits for no man in this world of ours, and it really doesn't matter who you are.

6-9-97
Planet

Waiting for the moment, that moment in time when the planet comes together in body, spirit, and mind. We will join together, no more race, color, or creed, we will join together in peace and harmony. The World will evolve in many different ways because of the energy we give back to the planet every single day.

The problems that we have, we will have no more, the positive energy will just seem to have opened up a door. Out with the bad and in with the good, this planet will be filled with peace, love, and brotherhood.

6-19-04
Playing the Game

The energy from the Universe, the energy from above, the energy from with in is nothing but love. This energy that I speak of, this energy from the stars, this energy from within has always been ours. We create with this energy, it is just a tool, we create with this energy anything and everything that we can really use.

Students, teachers, it is all the same, the energy comes to those who know how to play the game. Love is created, hate is too, friendship is created by this energy that we use.

6-16-02
Poor Me

When something happens, when something goes wrong, people seem to play poor me until the day is gone. It was your choice, your actions too, that put you in this predicament, now it's all up to you. This world is crazy, or so it would seem, so many people with so many dreams.

Believe in yourself, the energy will arrive, and it will take you on a fantastic ride, your ups, your downs, they won't mean a thing, as long as you have this energy, you can have anything. The time is now, the energy has come, and it's here for each and every one.

2-10-98
Positive Thinking

Positive thinking puts you in control of the subconscious mind known as the ego. It doesn't really matter what you think or do, positive thinking will guide you too.

Insight and coincidence will begin to grow as your positive thinking puts you in control. The problems that seemed so hard to do will instantly become natural for you. The power of the Universe, it can be yours, all you have to do is open up that door. Many people will never understand, we all have this power, it's born in every man.

By Jim Lozen

12-23-99
Potential

The mind is incredible, and it's born in every man, but man doesn't seem to use it, so he'll never understand. "FREE YOUR MIND!" The body is a prison that you don't really need, because we are nothing but pure energy.

The world around you, the mountains, and the streams are just molecules and neutrons, they are also energy. This Global planet that we live on, that we call Earth is just an illusion that we have had since birth.

Beliefs are something that we have set in our mind, and we have had them for all eternity of something that we call mankind.

Free your spirit, do whatever you can, and reach for the potential that's in every man.

12-13-98
Quantum Leap

I am who I am and who I want to be at this moment in time, I create my own reality. The choices are there, the decisions are mine, and it's the only thing that will affect the outcome in time. Life is a circle, a rope if you will, that has no end and never will.

Your Reality is something that you create with every thought and breath that you take. Every decision and every choice that you make will affect someone else in this LIFE that you make. Life is ETERNAL, something that has no end, it's like taking a QUANTUM Leap over and over again.

8-2-97
Power of God

It doesn't matter what your name is, it doesn't matter who you are, the flow of energy is within your grasp, and it doesn't matter who you are. You create every day of your life with the energy from within, the energy that surrounds this planet is all you need to begin.

Your thoughts are just like building blocks, the power comes from your mind, anything that you can think of, you can have, and it's always been that way for all of mankind. This has become a "show me" world, people won't believe what they can't see, but in your mind is the power of God, and we all have this, and it's as easy your ABCs.

By Jim Lozen

Power

The power inside is the power of the man, and the people of the Earth just don't seem to understand. The power I'm talking about is the power of the mind, with it, you can do anything at any given time. Look at Franklin, Edison, and Ford, they all had this power, it's not something that is brand new, all you have to do is think, and this power will come to you.

God gave us all a gift that we don't really know how to use, we're afraid to use it in public, because we're afraid of ridicule.

10-22-2000
Prayer

Positive thinking, it's just like a prayer, it releases the power that's in the air. The energy that surrounds us, the energy within is the power that you use, that's how it begins. The power of the universe, the power in a man is just the energy he holds within his hand.

Everything has this power, everything under the Sun, the power is inherent in each and every one. The power, it's in the oceans, the power, it's in the trees, it's also in the flowers, the air, and the breeze. This power is universal, it's born to every man, but the people of the Earth, they just don't seem to understand.

Predator

Time is a predator, and there's nothing you can do, it's like a full blown virus, and it's coming after you. When age creeps up, it slows you down, but time speeds up, and it's still coming around.

I wish I could stop this thing called time, because after all, it's just in your mind.

When you're raised as a child, you're taught to tell time, so it becomes a factor in your mind. There's a time for peace, a time for love, and a time to look to the heavens above.

2-27-2000
Priest

Give us your money and do it right away, or we'll send you to Satan, and we'll do that today. We can do that, God made us the "MAN," but you stupid people, you just don't seem to understand. We're here to enlighten you, that's what we say, but we need more money in that COLLECTION plate today.

God don't like poor folk, he said this once before, he wants his Priests looking good when they get out on the floor. Give us your money, and you'd better do it right away, because we're giving a free pass to Heaven, but we're only doing that today.

3-07-95
Problems

I've got problems running through my mind, problems that I can get rid of but only for a very short time.

I'll go to the dojo and work out every night, takes care of my problems and that's all right, but when I get tired and go back home, they seem to creep back in when I'm all alone.

Problems will be the death of me, because you can't fight what you can't see.

5-17-03
Program

The program has already been written, but the choice, it's still yours, but you will find the choice that you have chosen, you have already chosen once before. Remember, the past is the future, the future is the past, what goes around comes around, and the "now" will always last.

The edge is the darkness, the darkness is time, but time only exists in one's own mind. Free your mind, and the light will come, evolution belongs to each and every one. We say there are three dimensions, but there are four or five, but you will never find them unless you free your mind.

7-11-95
Proof

I've been proving myself ever since I was a kid, proving myself in everything that I did. People won't accept you when you have a defect in life, it's hard to get a job and make a good life. I'll stay on my own, I don't have many friends, people like me are doomed till the end.

5-24-97
Protector

He stands out in this field all alone, he protects this land, but he is on his own. He is the critical mass from each one of us that have grown, the critical mass, but he is still on his own. Each one of us that joins him gives him a little more power, and soon, the critical mass will begin to devour, and soon, the people of the World will begin to see that the future ahead isn't what it was projected to be.

The energy that's out there, it's free for all of mankind, all we have to do is teach them to use it before we become one for all of time, then this World can be like it was meant to be, no evil upon it, just filled with loving energy.

9-16-01
Proud to Be an American

Proud to be an American, proud to live this way, proud to be an American until my dying day. Generations before us, our Mothers and our Dads fought to keep this freedom alive in all the wars we had. Our Nation is in trouble, lives are the price, we'll have to pay to keep our way of life here in the USA.

Proud to be an American, proud to lay it all on the line, proud to be an American and march into Hell at any given time. Freedom is a cost that we will never pay, freedom is a way of life here in the USA.

1-19-97
Pushed It

You'll never change, you are who you are, and there's no turning back again, because you've pushed it too far! People told me from the start that you couldn't be changed, but I couldn't believe that deep down in my heart. I should have guessed, I should have known that they were right, because nothing's working out for me, at least not tonight.

Times have changed within the last five years, I keep evolving, and the old Jim seems to have disappeared, but you haven't changed, you haven't changed a bit, I guess the good book's right when it says God loves an Idiot.

It takes all kinds to fill this world of ours, and you're just one of them who has pushed it too far!

5-16-98
Rosy Red

Rosy red and indigo, the colors of the mind, will not change the way you think throughout your whole lifetime.

My mind is a warehouse that no one will ever see, it's filled to the rim with insight and intuition, and it's just for me. It's the only thing I'll ever own, it's the only thing I will ever need, this intuition and insight, and it's God-given ability.

6-14-96
Rain

There's thunder in the background, lightning from above, soon, the rains will come to nurture the Earth with nothing but love.

The rains will feed the land, the flowers, and the trees, and they in turn will give us the air that we breathe.

If man cuts all the trees down, and the flowers, they don't grow, what's going to give us the energy to make our bodies go?

7-2-2000
Reality, Yes or No

This isn't reality, it's all in your mind, we came here to experience the life that we couldn't find. Reality is the dream that we have now and then, because we are just spirits until the very end. We inhabit these bodies, or should I say tools, to experience the life that otherwise we couldn't do.

A winter's day, a summer's eve, the heat of the desert, or the cool ocean breeze, these are the things that we came here to do, and when we are done, we will all come back to you.

It doesn't really matter, because it's all just in your mind, reality doesn't exist, at least not in this lifetime.

7-13-02
Rebirth

Everything I have, everything that I need is just an illusion that I materialize naturally. Over the years, the centuries too, we have been domesticated, me and you. You have to realize in order to see that this world is just an illusion for you and me. The reality of this planet, the reality at this time are the beliefs of many thousands of people, many thousands of minds.

The energy of this planet, the energy of our mind is the energy of the universe and will be here until the end of time. You can't destroy this, evolution is just a tool, the making of this planet is and was for me and you.

12-11-99
Recall

We all have a power that's born inside of you, but it's something we have never been taught, so it's something we never use. It's the power to go back in time, the power to manifest a previous lifetime.

Life is an Illusion, it doesn't matter what you think or say, life is an Illusion that you make up along the way. Desire your Outcome, and as the actions, they come your way, make the right choices, and the World is yours this very day.

8-31-96
Reincarnation

God is here, he's in your mind, he's what you make him out to be for all time. There's no Heaven above us, there's no Hell below, God is with you everywhere you go. You might die today, but you don't really die, you just enter a higher plain of evolution in your mind, then you're reborn again in some other place and time to start all over again in some other lifetime.

2-25-2000
Reject

It takes money to live here in this backward place, these little green bills they call dollars are cherished by the human race. You won't believe this, but they still have time, and as we all know, time is just a belief that is in your mind.

Their belief system, it's all wrong, we are going to have to change this before we can let them come along. They still believe that might makes right, and every time that you turn around, some other country is getting into a fight! I give up, there's nothing I can do, so I'm coming home, buddy, I'm coming back with you.

3-8-2000
Relationships

Life is a relationship, a meeting of the minds that will guide you to the next level, the next level in time. Time is evolution, evolution is time, and if you go stagnant, you will be here forever if only in your mind!

Develop the mind, because that is the key, develop the mind, and evolution is the next step for humanity. Love is the answer, but the mind is the key, they have told us this for generations, but we have yet to see.

If we could only listen with our hearts for just a little while, we could build up on this planet such a beautiful lifestyle. The planet would rejoice, evolution would give us everything that we need, and we would live forever in a common reality.

2-24-01
Relaxation

Total relaxation, "God's" gift to man, we call it hypnotism, but we don't seem to understand. It's the energy around us, the power within that starts us on this journey as our mission begins. We choose our own life, we choose our missions too, with the help of this force, this energy we use.

Everything that happens, we created with our mind, and it will appear at some point in the rivers of time. Everything you "need, want, and desire" too is accomplished through this energy that we just happen to use.

Relax, "focus on the deed," and the answers will come to you, the answers you need. We are all equal, we are all but one, and as soon as we can realize this, the journey has begun.

8-13-97
Remember

Things that you were taught in school are not things you didn't know but things you don't remember from so very long ago. Lives you have lived seem so very far away, but your teachers are just trying to remind you of the things you knew that day.

We were all once warriors, potentates, and kings, but where we are now in life, that doesn't mean a thing. The past is our future, the future is our past, and with each life, we evolve, our world will always last. It might not be on the same planet, it might be out there amongst the stars, it doesn't really matter, because you'll always be who you are.

8-31-96
Responsibility

Everyone wants it, but no one wants to take the blame, but they'll take the credit all the same. I've always wanted responsibility to make my life turn out the way I want it to be.

All your life, you were taught to think the way that others do, they taught you to conform when you were in school, and if you varied from that line, you were considered an outcast for all time.

The Church, they teach you to obey by brainwashing you every step of the way. Power corrupts, an absolute power corrupts absolutely, they're trying to crush our creativity, so no one's responsible for anything anymore, we're just a bunch of sheep to be led and nothing more.

6-17-2000
Resurrection

I'm tired of sleeping without you, I'm tired of calling your name, since you left a month ago, things aren't quite the same. The memories of the life we had come flooding back "EVERY SINGLE DAY" by certain little things I do or things that I might just happen to say.

With the energy around us, I know you haven't really gone, you just finished your mission in life and decided to move on. I know where to find you every week or every day in Resurrection Cemetery up the hill right off the bay.

9-23-01
Retaliation

You're with us or against us, or we can do this all alone, because this is America and this is our home. Remember the Alamo, remember the Maine, remember the Towers, it's all the same. We're coming to get you, and you don't know when, but we're coming to get you and put this to an end.

The lady is in the harbor, she stands all alone, weeping for the children that she has known. Islam is with us, Turkey is too, the Muslim nations are behind us in whatever we do. We won't back down, we have the might, an attack on American soil has given us the right.

We'll fight for freedom, we'll fight for the cause, you have awoken the sleeping Tiger, and now you have lost.

9-2-99
Revolution

In another life at some other point in time, I was a writer in a former lifetime. I wrote for freedom, I wrote for the cause, I wrote for the people who had no voice at all. I wrote of each battle the blood and the gore, I wrote of Liberty and of the people who wanted more.

I wrote to John Adams and Tom Jefferson too, I told them of the glory that they were taking us to. The time had come for every woman and man to tell the British that this was our land.

Heroes were dying, Martyrs were being born, in the first few pages of History, America was already torn.

5-20-2000
Riddles

Life is eternal, we can never die, the spirit within is the reason why. All of your desires, wants, and needs are just one step away in your reality. Your reality changes from day to day because of your wants and things that you happen to say.

Your mind is eternal, and that is the key, because your mind is nothing but pure energy. Energy dwindles throughout the day, and you sleep to restore what you cannot save. Dreams are clues, riddles of the mind by which the spirit speaks to us and does all of the time.

12-21-97
Road Kill

Racing down the highway, driving down the road in my Saturn '93, eating road kill as I go. I'll be home for Christmas, you can count on me, I'll be bringing Christmas dinner, it's in the trunk of my Saturn '93.

I think I'll start a restaurant after the Holidays, put it by the side of the road and call it the "Road Kill Cafe." We can find our dinners any time of the day along that stretch of the road they call the highway.

I can make a bundle with this idea of mine, selling exotic foods to the public, and it won't cost me a dime.

4-7-96
Roller Coaster

I've had quite a life in my forty-five years, I've done what I've had to to put everything in the right gear.

Life has its ups and downs, it's like a roller coaster, and you keep going around, but you can't give up, and you can't get off, because people who do are sure to get lost.

I've had a few setbacks, but I've never turned to drugs or booze, because if you turn to them, you are sure to lose.

You have got to stay in the right frame of mind, then life will be easy half of the time.

5-26-03
Survive

We are energy, each and every one, the energy from this planet, the stars, and even the sun. Light has no ending, and darkness hasn't a clue, domestication has brought this to both me and you.

Beliefs are the culprit, the brainwash has taken its toll, but the truth of the matter is that we will never grow old! Energy can't be destroyed, it can only be transformed, and this is the only reason that you were even born. To populate this planet, to make it come alive, with this energy, we will always survive.

11-28-96
Santa Claus

He's at the North Pole, he works every day, and then on Christmas Eve, he loads his sleigh. He makes his rounds to every town, and he comes down the chimney when no one is around. Little is known about this guy except he has reindeer that seem to know how to fly.

He does all his work in just one day, he doesn't have time to talk, and he doesn't have time to play. He's a toy maker, at least that's what I hear, he's been making these toys for quite a few years.

He's known by many names, the country worldwide, but he's still the great gift bringer, and from that, he cannot hide. Santa is a feeling, it doesn't matter which name he goes by, he's just a feeling that we all have deep down inside.

3-19-2000
Satan

Tomorrow is the future, and yesterday is the past, but today is "Now," and the now will always last. There is no present in the future, there is no time in the past, time was conjured up by man to make a moment last. The "Ego" is the devil, the devil of all of mankind, and the only place he will ever exist is in the valleys deep within the mind.

We all have one thing in common, we all have an ego all of our own, and most of these egos are definitely "homegrown!" The ego is Unconscious, the ego doesn't seem to know, but the ego is our own little "SATAN" from the depths below.

Scholar

I'm not the scholar that I would like to be, but I'm like the Army, I'm the best I can be, there was a time when I was like you, I would mess up, and I would just try to make do, age and experience has overcome that, and I can surly put everything on the right track.

Kids nowadays want the big bucks, and if you're in the way, it's just your tough luck, they take a giant step before they can crawl, and if we don't look out, it will be the end of us all.

I admit it's probably our fault, because we taught them from childhood that money's the boss, if you don't have money, you don't have anything, money in America is the King.

8-15-96
School

Time is speeding up as the years go by, and the memories that come with it makes you stop and wonder why.

You could have done better, but you didn't even try, if you're like most people, you'll just blame it on some other guy. Education is where it's at, you don't have anything if you don't have that.

My education ended with High School, I wish I would have gone farther now, but I was too cool.

I hung out with the in crowd back then, because I was cool way back when, now I'm paying the price for being too cool, I was stupid, I should have stayed in school.

3-11-95
Searching

I've been searching for a woman for such a long time, searching for a woman whom I can call mine.

I've been looking for this woman in every town, I go looking for this woman I don't even know.

I've been worried about spending my life all alone, worried about having no place to call home.

I've been searching for a woman for such a long time, searching for a woman whom I can call mine.

10-13-96
Seasons

The seasons are changing, the days are getting cold, another year is ending, and you're another year old. What have we done to change this world of ours, to make things better than they are. This world won't change on its own, we have got to do it, and we are all alone.

The bureaucrats won't help us, they're just out for some quick cash, we have got to do this to make our future last. People look out for just number one, but we have got to stick together to get anything done, let's make a resolution to help each other if we can, then this world will be a better place for each and every man.

3-9-99
Secrets

The power of the Pyramids, the energy of the Stars helped to form this planet and make us who we are.

Orion's belt in the Universe and our Sister Planet Mars both were once inhabited with people from the Stars. They came here on a mission that no one seems to know, but the Secrets are buried in the Arctic under Tons and Tons of snow.

One day, we will discover the Secrets of Mankind and unlock the Powers and the Secrets of the Mind.

By Jim Lozen

9-4-03
Seven Years

Seven year's difference between my brother and me, I was considered the kid until I was twenty-three. He always took my side when I was small, with my brother right by me, I felt ten feet tall.

He finished college in '62 with a master's degree and one in business too! He settled down in Grand Rapids and made a life with his dog named Butch and Karen, his wife. He never had any kids to call his own, so he adopted mine so he would never be alone.

He's retired now but still consults whenever he can for the big bucks, because he's the man!

Shape-Shifters

We are all but energy blowing in the wind, shifting shapes, and that's how the story begins. You can't destroy us, our bodies will die, but the energy within will give life another try! We shift shapes, travel in many forms, and then eventually when the time is right, a new child is born. We have this power that many people wouldn't even begin to understand, the power is the light that's born to every man.

The light is an Aura, a beacon of such that draws teachers to us until we have been taught enough to complete the mission, to reach our goals, then the light takes over and shows us the way home. We learn by experience every single day, we learn from our mistakes in much the same way.

10-24-98
Signature

My truth is filled with lies from the beginning to the end, you have to figure them all out before you can call me a friend. Friendship is a dying breed, if your friends just use you until they get what they need.

A Thunderous Silence came out from the cold as the years went by and I grew old. Four years of service, four years of time, three years of pain that shouldn't be mine. In the wrong place at the right time, or is it all just an Illusion that has passed through my mind?

7-31-96
Single Mom

She gets up every morning at five and goes to work, because she's just trying to keep her family alive. She has three little kids depending on her, she raises them kids and never says a word.

Her ex ran out when she was twenty-two, left her with three kids, and never paid a cent to help her make it through. She raises the kids the best she can and doesn't need any help, especially from a man.

9-28-02
Sixty Years

A parallel universe where we are all one, where we have come together under the morning's hot sun. September 11th was just such a day, December 7th was much the same way. Sixty years have come and gone, sixty years before anyone knew something was wrong.

Wrong or right, right or wrong doesn't matter whose side you're on, what you do to him, you do to me, when will this world finally see. Mothers packing lunches for boys who won't return, both sides have it, and both sides have been burned. A parallel universe where we are all the same, a parallel universe where we are all insane.

3-28-02
Solutions

Everything that I choose, I choose through you, everything that I see, I make part of me. The oceans, the flowers, and the trees were all created by people like me. Negative thinking will create the unknown, it is inevitable, and this is how fear has grown.

The story of the warrior and the king both have solutions to them and happy endings. Life is just a story, the solutions are few, the choices are many, it all depends on you. You are responsible for whatever you do, you are the writer in your book of who's who.

The story continues each and every day, the story of life and the games people play.

11-22-95
Someone

I'm losing you, baby, and I don't know why, I'm losing you, darling, and it's making me cry.

You're the only one who's ever meant something to me, you're the only one who could set me free.

You have always been there when I needed you, you have always been there to help me get through.

But where are you now that I need you the most? I've looked around, but you're nowhere to be found.

Someone to talk to, someone to hold, someone to cuddle with when the nights get cold.

10-8-2000
Soul Mates

Tell me your desires, tell me your needs, I have two arms to hold you, and I am ready to please! Fate brought us together, fate took us by the hand, fate will take us places that we will never understand. Free will and choices, it's all up to you, you are the "Goddess of Love," and I am just one name in your book of "Who's Who."

Fate brought us together, and we will stay that way for all time, because free will and choices are yours and mine. The days may come, and the days may go, but soul mates like us, we will never grow old.

12-3-99
Space and Time

The Past is behind you, it's something that you can't see, but it's there nonetheless, it's part of your reality. The future is before you, some people call it your destiny, but you've been there and done that, it's also reality.

The Past, Present, and Future, there just a space and time that you have the power to channel through the valleys of the mind. You know what's going to happen deep within your mind, so why not just use this power and let the journey unwind .

6-24-01
Space

The end of illusion, the end of time, the end of space resides within your own mind. Space doesn't exist without a form, and this planet never was until you were born. We are all cogs in this wheel, and we have different perceptions on how we all should feel. Life is energy that can't be destroyed, and illusion is reality that's in every girl and boy

The future is time, the past is too, but the moment is now, and that's all we will ever use. Problems are yours, they're not mine, because problems don't exist in the present time. Don't look to the past where your problems reside, don't look to the future on the other side, the time is now, the future has come, and it's been born into each and every one.

3-29-98
Species

Wants are in the future, needs are in the past, beliefs are in the present, and time will always last. This World keeps turning, there's always a plan for each and every child, woman, or a man.

Things that have happened, things that you have done have touched someone's life, and without you, none of these things could have been done. Each life that we live, each piece of the puzzle that we solve makes way on this planet for our species to evolve.

By Jim Lozen

4-14-97

Spirit Within

I don' t know where I'm going, I don't even know who I am, but the spirit inside will guide me just like he does for any other man. The energy that's out there, the energy within will make my decisions for me through gut feelings and intuition.

The negative energy is all but gone, and the positive energy is coming on strong. My life has changed in the last two years, my old life just seems to have disappeared.

Energy is all that you will ever really need, the energy from the sun, the stars, and the trees. Nature, that is the key, it will give you all the energy that you will ever need.

11-26-96

Spirit

I believe in myself, I believe in who I am, and I believe in the spirit that's born in every man. He animates your body, he defines just who you are, and with this spirit as part of your life, he will help you to see just who you are.

He helps you when you're troubled, you'll know just what to do, you'll have insights and inspiration, because that's what spirits do. Let your mind go, let the spirit within come to the top as your story begins.

Start your life over, become as one of us, let your spirit guide you through, but that isn't quite good enough, you've got to let the ego go before your transformation is done, then we'll join together, and we will become as one.

12-3-2000
Star Wars

Energy and thinking, they work hand in hand, but positive energy is one thing that people just don't seem to understand. The life force is energy, thinking is too, feelings are energy, and that's all part of you. "Negative energy," it will bring you right down, make you sick, and eventually put you six feet underground.

Love is the secret, love is the energy that flows, love is the answer to the question that everybody knows. The love for a puppy, the love for a child, the love for a car is just love that will last for a little while. The energy that they produce is used by you and me, and this energy will remain for all eternity.

Obi-Wan was right when he said that this force belongs to you and me, he was also right when he said that there were two kinds of energy.

2-12-2000
Star

It's your World, you're the star, the other people are just characters or supporting actors, it doesn't matter who they are! Everything that you desire becomes part of this play, all of your choices are written in the script that way. You follow the directions to the tee, you never make a mistake, because you are me.

The mistakes you make are written into the play, because that is the choice that you made today. When the play is over and the finale curtain comes down, you will have time to reflect before another play comes around.

Streets

I was in love with this girl once upon time, we got along real good, and that was just fine, then something happened, it came out of the blue, she fell in love with another guy, and I was through.

For a while there, I tried to win her back, but then I found out I was headed up the wrong track, it didn't really matter that much to me, because all I wanted was a friend that I could see, and if anything happened other than that, I was pretty sure I could handle that, but it didn't, and I lost again, so I'm back in the streets where it all began.

5-26-97
Thank You, God

Thank you, God, for the things that you do, thank you, God, for the experiences that you put me through. I wouldn't know what this World is like without your help to get me through the night.

You have got to learn love before you can hate, you have got to learn to destroy before you can create. I didn't know what this life was all about until I met you and you turned my life inside out. There's an opposite reaction for everything that you do, so just be careful about the things that you choose. That's what we were all put here for, to learn these experiences and nothing more.

1-17-2000
Take My Power, PLEASE!

Deep purple and violet blue, these are some of the colors that I see in you. Energy from the Universe, energy from the stars, it's energy from the planets that makes you who you are.

You don't need an Education, you don't need to go to school, because the energy from the universe will bring out the power that's inside of you. We are all God's children, and that is the KEY, if we are all God's children, then the power is already inside of me!

Religion tells you one thing, and they tell you what not to do, but that's so they can take your power and have power over you!

Over the Millennium and as time goes by, your power diminishes, and the people, they wonder why.

3-5-2000
Teach the Children

You already know the answer, the answer is you and me, and we have to bring this planet together by using its own energy. Nobody said this would be easy, but nobody said this would be hard. We have already done this in the future, and we have already done this in the past, so we'll do it again right here and now, and the now will always last.

There is no time in the future, but there is no future in the time, time is but a belief that man conjured up in his mind. If we could teach the people on this planet everything that we know, the energy on this planet would just seem to grow, grow, and grow.

3-20-96
Teacher

Some people call me a teacher, they say I speak through the written word, but if no one reads my writings, what have I accomplished, what have they heard? If I could tell people all the things that life has taken me to, maybe they could avoid a few of the mistakes life has taken me through.

I can't speak very clearly, most people don't understand, so I'll just keep on writing my rhymes and doing the best that I can.

4-24-97
Tears

She had tears in her eyes as she spoke to me. I could tell that she was going through some pain that wouldn't set her free. The loss of a loved one, so much pain and so many memories, these were the feelings that she was sending to me.

I wished I could have helped her, I wished she would have opened up to me, and then I could have given her some of my energy. Energy from the planet that helps us know right from wrong, energy from the Universe that helps us grow oh-so-strong. These are what I would have given to her, but she wouldn't open up, she wouldn't say a word.

2-19-2000
The Journey

The path is filled with stones and rocks and boulders to block the way, but you must have the inspiration and insight to move them from the path today. Know that you know, and they all just fade away, life is that easy, it's the mind that makes it hard, you have to free the mind to find out who you really are.

Your mind is like a computer that needs to be defragged because of the old beliefs that you don't use any longer and you don't need anyway. Delete it, make backups if you wish, because in your present life, you don't need any of this.

9-19-98
The Bible

The Bible, it's fiction, a book of dreams, unless you can decipher the code and find out just what it means. Mary is the mother, the planet Earth, and Joseph is the Sun for what it's worth. Twelve Disciples, you can call them by name, Twelve Zodiac signs in the sky, to me, they're both the same.

Christ died on the cross, or so they say, the Earth dies every Fall and sleeps through Winter's day. Coincidence one and all, you believe what you want or nothing at all.

2-25-2000
The Calling

This is the way that it was supposed to happen, this was the way I was supposed to find out about you. "I'm sorry it took so long, I'm not that smart," but my body is dormant, and I am going to live forever now that I know what I am supposed to do.

Bring the world and its people together with every thought and dream that I can make come true. Teach them the love that surrounds this planet, teach them the love that is really you. You're the winds that blow, you're the oceans that rise, you're everything from outside and inside.

10-5-02
The Change

In a different universe, in a different time when I was once yours and you were once mine. Reincarnation, the name of the game, reincarnation, where we were all once the same. Negative energy, negative vibes have taken us apart, so we aren't you and I.

We built the pyramids, we built the great wall, we fought in the Alamo and died one and all. The times they keep changing, they change every day, but the energy of life, it remains the same way. When will this universe finally see and get back together for all eternity.

6-11-2000
The Door

Trapped in a body, locked in a mind, searching for the light at the end of time. The door to perception is the exact same way, but we have the key to open that today.

Beyond the door is a new reality that will open up to man's curiosity. Christ is Judas, Judas is he, we are all but one in this reality. The colors of the ocean, the colors of the sea, it doesn't really matter, because they are both just like me. We are all one in this new reality, and it will be ours for all eternity.

The Creator of the sun, the Creator of the stars made us all alike no matter who we are. The showers from the Heavens, the Heavens above fill this land with his eternal Love.

4-29-2000
The Key

You only have one life unless you're like me, an immortal in this world of humanity. I have been here before, this is nothing new for me in this world of ever-changing reality. The world is but an Illusion, the people are but pawns in every dimension that I have ever lived on.

Dimension is time, time is eternity, because it doesn't exist as part of me. The bending of the light, which you call time, is really the evolution of the mind. The body is dormant, but you have the key, and with it, you create your own reality.

2-2-97
The Man

Problems are nothing, there just in your mind. Get out there and interact with other people, and they'll help you out all of the time. This world's an easy place to live in, everything is right there, all you have to do is find it, but people don't care.

They think that money is the answer, but little do they know money just corrupts, it doesn't help the energy flow. All you need is the energy from the colors and the trees, and God will do the rest, he'll give you anything you need. He helps you out through insight and inspiration when he can, and with him by your side, you can't find a better man.

12-31-02
The Matrix

Free your mind, let it go free, this thing they call the matrix, it has a hold on me. Walking zombies, soldiers one, two, three, have created this world for people just like you and just like me. Imagination has gone, negativity has set in, when all we have to do is open our minds to let the journey begin.

Everything I think, say, or do, I create, and so do you. This world is funny, because nobody seems to understand that this world was created for every single man.

The canvas is blank just as it was the night before, it's waiting for love to create and so much more. We have all of this power that nobody seems to know how to use, but it's just waiting for someone, someone like you.

The Outsiders

They came from the planets, they came from the stars, they came from the heavens to show us just who we are. They came down to Earth in such a fascinating way, they came as the energy we use every day.

Our ideas are not always are own, although we will take the credit, we didn't do it alone. The cosmic energy that surrounds and upholds will one day begin to unfold.

The people will begin to realize that we are not alone, but by then the enlightenment of this planet will already have grown.

3-3-2000
The Painting

This is only energy, this pencil that I hold, but it is the energy of this planet that we have created with since days of old. The energy never changes, the energy is always the same, but our perception of this planet changes because it's all just part of the game. We create with an illusion that certain people can see, and this illusion soon becomes part of our reality.

The colors of this planet are also the colors of the mind, and these are the color's that we have created with since the beginning of time. Life is like an easel that we paint on from day to day, you paint your own reality in the exact same way.

11-7-99
The Sting

Religion is sacred most people say, but the people of the World, they made it that way. Religion was put here by man one day, to control the people in what they said was a spiritual way.

Two thirds of this planet doesn't even know God exist, does that mean that they're all going to hell when we get through with this? He is the energy around us, He is the Stars and the Sun, He is within us all, He is everyone.

4-1-01
The Best

I know that being here with you was the best thing that I could ever do, seeing right from wrong are only feelings that are going on. In my mind, I can see the colors of this planet and my very own reality.

The energy that I have within makes me grow as the day begins, the colors that I see help to guide this reality, turns it all around even turns it upside down. The day is gone, that you brought to me, the time is now for all eternity, I wish I knew the rules so I could play this game of life that we play every day.

In the valley, I can see the dreams of life that come so naturally, but I don't know when to start, when to leave, or when to part, so I will play this game alone until the valley turns to stone.

3-26-2000
The Colors of the Stars

The colors of the Universe, the colors of the stars, the colors of the people define just who they are. The energy from this planet doesn't mean a thing without the colors from the Universe and the life it seems to bring. Everyone has a color that seems to change from night to day, it all depends on which kind of mood they are in, which brings out the colors in this way.

The color red, which is born to every child, is the color of a negative thinker that will last for just a little while. Teach the children, that's what we have to do, teach the children and change that color to Crimson or Blue.

The Creator

You create your own life, you create your death too, you create everything and anything that happens to you. The choices you make, the decisions you choose all rolled into one, it's the real you. The illusions of this planet, the illusions of time are all rolled up into one, one's own mind.

You see what you want, you see what you need, then you create, because this is your reality .When the time is now and the future is here, death and destruction will simply disappear.

3-11-01
The Dark Side

The dark side comes from out of your past and into the present, where these feelings will just seem to always last. Feelings are energy, and so are you, this energy you are feeling, you have already used. Past life experience, or could be a future one too, this energy you are expelling is called "déjà vu."

Each thought that passes, each trickle of time, you never stop creating from within the mind. Anything that you want or desire too can be had for the thought that's inside of you.

The dark side will be over, all things must pass, when we learn to love ourselves, the "NOW" will always last. The future is ours, the past is too, the moment is now, but it's all up to you.

3-28-99
The End of the World

I have all I want now! I have everything that I need, at this moment in time now, I am the Master of my own Destiny. Sometimes I'm happy, sometimes I'm so blue, it all has to deal with the choices I choose. You create with your mind now, each moment of the day. You create with your thoughts and words that you say.

We're God's gift to the World now! You and me, because without us now, the World would cease to be.

11-10-2000
The Energy Within

The energy is out there, the energy is just for you, all you have to do is learn to use this energy, and it will come to you. I'm not here to teach you, I don't think I could even if I tried, because the energy you seek is the energy inside.

The Mountain has a rocky pass, the valleys are deep but low, the rivers that you must cross are all rivers that you will know. The centuries have come and gone, but the energy within will never move on. Look for tomorrow, but tomorrow will never come, and search for the energy at the dawn of the setting sun.

3-24-01
The Force

Feelings are energy, the energy within, feelings are the force, and you're the way it all begins. There is no wrong or right, no devil below, there is only this force that we will all but one day know. The energy from this planet, the energy from the stars, the energy from this universe defines us and shows us who we really are.

The force is always with you, the force came out of your past, the force is with you now, and the force will always last. Follow your desires , follow your dreams, freedom of choice will give you everything. This world is an illusion, you can do whatever it is that you want to do, all you have to do is imagine, and this world belongs to you.

3-7-2000
Forgotten Land

You choose your own life, and then you make a plan before you even come down here, so you will better understand. You pick your own experiences, you're on your own, and when it comes to facing them, you're all alone.

Choose the right path, and life becomes easy for you, there's nothing you will ever have trouble with, and there's nothing you can't do. Choose the wrong path, and life becomes unbearable for you, you're always running into obstacles, and life becomes impossible to do.

There is no "Right" or "Wrong," so it doesn't really matter which path you choose, because all you have to do is change your thinking and it really isn't that hard to do. Go with the flow, do what you will, because the energy will actually guide you to the top of the Hill! On the other side is the land that you sought, the land that you thought time had forgot.

5-4-03
The Future Past

There is no Devil, there is no sin, what you create happens to him. Him is you, him is him, you create your own reality, and that isn't a sin. We create whatever happens to me and you, we create whatever happens by the choices we choose.

The "Big Bopper," he died in '51 by the flip of a coin, his choice affected everyone. The choices you make, the reality you choose, this is for everyone, even me and you.

5-16-99
The Gathering

Feelings are energy, and energy is the power that will take you to the limits of your Desire. Everything has this, everything under the stars has the ability to find out just who or what you are.

Focus on your feelings or focus on the stars to find the inner self and learn what kind of person you really are. I thought I was a Madman seeing colors all the time, but the colors, they turned out to be just the rivers of the mind, if I can do this, you can do it too, just know that this will happen, and before you know it, it will happen to you.

2-20-2000
The Second Coming

The Ego is a trip that you don't need, because he is blocking the light from the Son and Me! We are all but brothers under the skin, walk a mile in his shadow and become part of him. Learn what you can, learn what you need, because we are all but one in reality. One with the planet, One with the man, One with each animal of this land.

"The Second Coming" we will find when the love that surrounds this planet is yours and mine. Thousands of years it will last, and there will be great advances that come from out of the past.

10-7-01
The Power of Now

The energy of this universe is our power to command, it belongs to each and every one us, only we don't seem to understand. The lives we've led in the centuries before are the clues we need to open each and every door.

We are all but energy, and energy can't be destroyed, we are all but energy that's in every girl and boy. There is no difference between us, we are all the same, there is no difference between us, and we have no one to blame.

We create our desires, we create all of our needs, we create with the "Power of Now" and this thing we call energy. We'll be here together in many different forms, because the energy of the Universe was ours since the day we were born.

3-19-2000
The Power of the Light

My life is changing daily, it's not the same anymore, whenever I get these feelings, my life suddenly changes from what it was before. Feelings are energy, "the Power of the Light" that can come at any time, even through the night. The light changes you, you're not the same man, we all have powers deep within that we just don't seem to understand.

The energy will guide you, it will even take you by the hand and lead you into what we would call the promised land. I have so much power in my mind that I would love to share with this world, but it really isn't mine! This is Evolution, and it belongs to you and me, the power of the light that we will all but one day see.

4-6-04
The Power of Thought

You create your future, you created your past too, because time doesn't exist without you. I change every day, I change all of the time, because this is my life and this reality is mine. I choose what I see, I see what I choose, because this universe is energy, the energy that I use. We all have this power, you and me, we all have this power and create everything that we see.

Praying works because of the energy that it makes, and positive energy is the energy that it creates. You created your own life, you'll create your death too, with this little thing that we call energy, the energy that we all use.

1-26-01
The Power to Create

Different cultures, different times, different realitys of the mind. Domestication or how you were raised will change this planet in many ways. You are an illusion, and our minds created all of this, and this illusion of the mind is the only reason that you exist.

"Think about it" for just a minute or two, think about the things that you or I can do. We have all of this power that we don't even understand, and with this power, we created this land. We created poverty, we created riches too, we created everything, because this power is inside of me and you.

10-13-2000
The Power Within

Decisions and choices, it depends on you, your destiny awaits, it depends on the choices you choose. My heart is open like a river that flows through the valleys to the canyons below. My directions are guided by my mind, it's true, but insight and inspiration are the powers I use.

Wrong or right doesn't exist for me, because I use the power of the Universe and all of its energy. We all have this power that we don't even understand, but the power of the Universe is yours to command. I breathe in "Reds, Yellows, Greens, and Blues," because these are the colors that I chose to use.

7-4-99
The Promised Land

We live in darkness, but we can see deep within our spirit is our destiny. The vehicle we travel in is only flesh and bone, but the Universal Consciousness has shown us that we are not alone.

The energy that surrounds this planet has been here for all time, all you have to do is learn how to use it, and you become part of that mind.

It isn't hard, evolution is at hand, and I look forward to the time when we cross over into that Promised land.

8-15-04
The Rode You Choose

I love you, babe, what more can I say than I love you, babe, each and every single day? You move the mountains, you move the seas when I'm with you and you're with me. Time stands still, or so it would seem, with you by my side, life is but a dream. We've created our future, we've created our past, with you my side, our love will always last.

Every minute, every second of the day, we've created a new life, and the old one has just simply faded away. The decisions you make and the choices you choose, the direction of life changes by the Path that you use.

1-06-96
Enough Time

I can't imagine living life without you, but now that it's happened, I'll make do. Living life with you was easy, and maybe I played it to cool when I should have been more worried about losing you.

Now I've got to find something to keep you off my mind, and I'll find that if I'm given enough time.

11-25-99
The Third Eye

Psychic phenomena and PSI, it's all there before you in your mind's eye. The third eye was a gift to man, the third eye will help you to better understand. Remote Viewing and the CIA, it was the wave of the future, and it still is today.

With the Electricity of the body and the Electricity of the mind, the things that will happen will happen right on time. No need to Worry, no need to Fret, this world keeps Chugging along and will get better yet.

11-15-95
The Band

I was off down the road, trying to find myself, looking for that inner man, Charlie, Andy, Dave, and I made up a touring band. We played in each and every town, and the people, they loved us, because they kept coming around.

We all had jobs during the day, because playing our music just didn't pay. I wrote a lot of the songs that we did, I've been into writing ever since I was a kid.

I was twenty-two, and we had seen the sights, we played a few gigs for a couple nights.

We were big way back when, but it's true, you can't go back again.

3-24-96
The Game

When life throws me a curve and I fall down, I get back up on my feet and keep moving along. If you give up, you'll give up again, and that's no way for me, because I'm out there to win.

It's the ninth inning, and the score's all tied, I either hit a homerun or give up and die. That's the way I've always been, I'm always out there, and I play to win.

When I get to the plate, I always have a strike against me, but I'm out there to win, so it really doesn't bother me.

7-10-95
The Wall

In the morning, I get there at the crack of dawn, it's so quiet and peaceful, there's nothing going on.

Standing in front of this big marble wall, thousands of names up on it that mean nothing at all, but all the memories from '68 and '69 that I can do without until the end of time.

This wall might mean a lot to people who weren't there, but for me, it brings back memories of a time I couldn't bear.

10-10-97
Thought

I stand five-foot-eight, I weigh 175, I've got blond hair and big blue eyes. The inner spirit has come to me, it's opened my eyes so I could see. I can see a lot of things that I have never seen before, it's like a whole new world, and I have just opened the door.

Time has no meaning in this new world of mine, I can be anywhere at any given time, it's like having a time machine, but then it's not, because I can do it with just a thought.

9-7-96
Thoughts

Your innermost Thoughts , the ones you hide from me, are the ones that I would most like to see. To know how you think, to know how you feel, to know how you deal with some problems that seem so real.

All these problems you create on your own with beliefs that you have had since you were grown.

Beliefs are something that are drummed into you by well-meaning parents that are doing the best that they can do. Beliefs can be changed, it's all up to you, just throw out the old and in with the new.

10-5-96
Three Little Kids

I've got these little children deep down in my heart, these three little kids that I've loved from the start. I'll always keep them deep down inside of me, where I can comfort and protect them like they were still here with me.

I remember way back when they used to come to me when they needed a friend. They're all grown up now, and I'm just a thing of the past , they only come to me now when they need some cash.

2-27-2000
Three Little Words

Three little words are always on my mind, every time I'm with you, which is most of the time. You're always there to help me no matter what I do, these three little words, they mean so much to you.

Throughout each century and every life I have ever had, you have always been there to guide and protect me when times were bad. I love how you do things, there's always a plan, even if it takes a Miracle before the people understand. "Help me, Jesus," are the only words I'll ever need, "Help me, Jesus," will set my soul and body free.

3-11-95
Throwaway Friend

Never been married, never had a wife, I've been a throwaway friend for nearly half of my life, women seem to use me till some other guy comes along, then they throw me away, they don't even tell me what went wrong. Now I'm not complaining, I'm not even asking why, I'm just saying it hurts to be that throwaway guy.

3-5-2000
Tick-Tock

This is a Tick-Tock world, although it really shouldn't be, because this is already the twenty-first century. The sands in the hourglass have mostly run out, but this world keeps turning as Science takes a long look about.

The age of Aquarius, the eleventh sign, the time of the thinker, or does it mean it's time to start using the mind? The mind is but a shadow that many people don't even understand, but it's the key to enlightenment in sharing this land. This world keeps turning as the sands keep running down, but will we find the answers before the last grain of sand touches ground?

10-21-98
Time after Time after Time

Death isn't scary if you can't die, and pain doesn't hurt you if you can't cry. It doesn't matter the color of your skin, Race is an Illusion that just matters to people like him.

We are just a Race of people with thoughts running through our minds, thoughts that keep changing with every single lifetime. Born once more upon this Planet in some other space and time, you are about to embark on some other lifetime. Maybe this time will be different, maybe this time you will be the Man, or maybe this time you'll just be a peasant, a man who tends the land.

5-4-97
Time after Time

I've been here time after time, I've been here, even though it's just been in my mind. I know the surroundings, I know what's over that hill, I know the people around here, even though I don't think I ever will.

The energy that's out there will enter our minds and do something different to us time after time. Time is different for every man, time is different, and we don't always understand.

The curve of the planet, the solar breeze, they both affect the energy that flows through me. I know what's going to happen, I can see it in my mind, I know what's going to happen, but I don't know the exact time. I've been here before time after time, I've been here before if only in my mind.

3-12-2000
Time for a Change

I am not going to get sick, I am never going to die, because I make my own beliefs, I am not like any other human guy. Beliefs make life happen, beliefs define just who you are, beliefs are what this worlds all about on this tiny little star.

It's the knowing that makes a belief come true, it's the knowing that's born inside of you. It's the knowing that will turn this world around, or it's the knowing that will turn it upside down. Beliefs have a way of coming true, because beliefs are the knowing that's inside of you. Make new beliefs, because it's time for a change, this worlds getting older, but it's still the same.

12-6-98
Time Has Left

Life after Death is what you believe until you see the light, no one can help you, not even me. We are but one, you and me, we are all part of God's life-giving ENERGY. The Sun comes up, the Moon goes down, the days seem to pass when no one's around. It doesn't matter what you believe, the AWAKENING will come to you just like it came to me.

Time seems to pass each and every day, but we are living in the NOW and that's where we will always stay. What you will do in the FUTURE you have already done in the PAST, what goes around comes around, the NOW will always LAST.

4-26-01

Time Is an Illusion

You see what you believe, and believe what you can see, we call this our reality, it's always changing from day to day, it changes at a moment's notice, and it will always be that way. Life is an illusion, we don't even exist, with our minds, we created all of this. We created the poor man, we created the rich man too, we created everything that we desired to do.

Time is an ocean created by man, an infinite part of this universe that he really doesn't understand. The waves of the ocean, the colors of the sea, we created all of this, and they are all part of me. The past is our future, the future is our past, we created this world so it would always last.

8-5-2000
Time Is on Your Side

There is no hate, hate doesn't exist, hate is purely just a Myth. Light and dark, opposites attract, therefore, you need love to bring hate back. Fear is dark, dark is light, love is the knowledge that comes through the night.

Evil is fear, a choice that you chose to believe, a choice that completes your present reality. This world is love in all different forms, because this world is the reality in which you were born. The future is yours, time is on your side, because time doesn't exist either, it just came along for the ride.

12-4-99
Time Machine

Meditation is easy, it's rather cut and dried, but if you go into thinking, your body will come inside. Be one with the Masters, be whatever it is that you want to be, stay with the Masters, and you will be just like me.

There's a Thousand Worlds on this planet, but there all on different plains, there's the Past, the Present, and the Future, but to me, they're all the same. I've been to the Birth of Christ, I've been to the Sea of Galilee, I've been all over this Planet in every Century. Time Machines are useless, Time Machines you'll never need, because we'll develop the power of the mind in the twenty-first century.

8-11-01
Time Waits for No Man

Time doesn't exist, and neither do we, we are an illusion of our own reality. Life is an illusion, reality is but a dream, this world of ours isn't quite as it would seem. We created this planet, we created the trees, we created the flowers, the sun, and the bees.

We create by desire, we create by the need, we create with the sun, the stars, and the sea. The energy upon this planet is all we will ever use, the energy within is part of me and you. The time is now and will always be, we have created this monster, and it has brought us right to our knees.

The choice is yours, the future is too, live in the now, because that's all you will ever need to use. No more aging, no more disease, because the time is now for you and me.

9-19-96
Utopia

Where life has fled, let it live again in some other space, some other time in the far reaches of the mind. Time has no meaning, in a field of energy, you can't destroy what you cannot see.

They're building better weapons all the time for the destruction of mankind , but they're fighting a battle that they can't win, because we'll all come back again. I've lived so many lifetimes, I've fought in so many wars that it's hard to believe that man hasn't learned from before.

One day, we'll get it right, and man will start living as he should, showing nothing but love and brotherhood. We'll build a Utopia here on Earth as it was meant to be, reaching out to help each other in peace and harmony.

8-13-98
Titanic

Two and a half miles below the sea stands a monument to the people of the twentieth century. She was built in Belfast, Ireland, for the White Star Line and sailed into history from Southampton for all time.

The people on board were just like you and me, each one had his or her own idiosyncrasies. April 14th, that fateful night, made heroes and heroines out of the people who lost that fight.

She is but a time capsule now for the world to see and know how we lived in the twentieth century.

1-12-03
To the Wind

Yesterday is gone, and tomorrow is on its way, but the time is now, and it is today. Problems don't arise, they never do, problems are created by people just like me and just like you. It's your choice and always will be, it's your choice, because this is your reality.

The environment you grew up in, the region, the country, the town, all played a major role in bringing your reality around.

It's a dirty job that must be done, one thought to the wind can change this planet for everyone. The universal consciousness can turn this planet upside down, or it can turn it topsy-turvy if love is all around. It's your choice and always will be, it's your choice, because this is your reality.

5-29-01
Today

This world is beautiful, or so it would seem , but this isn't real, it's only a dream. You don't know this, you're only a child, you have to grow with in the Centuries for just a little while. I've been here before, this isn't the first time, and every time I've been here, I've lived within the mind.

Time isn't happening, time isn't real, you created time out of necessity so how does that make you feel? Feelings are energy, and energy is who you really are, the energy of this planet, the moon, and the stars.

We are all one is what I am trying to say, we are all one, and the time is today.

8-5-01
Together, on Your Own

I am you, and you are me , we are all just energy together. Sunlight from the days that pass, rivers of the night that will always last together. I am you, and you are me, and we are all humanity together. Rotten pictures on the wall, the negative vibrations that come to us all, because we're together.

Energy is a solo act, you have to learn on your own so you can act together The energy from this planet and the energy from the sun act as a team that is born to each and every one together. This planet is part of you, the sunlight and the oceans too, together. The energy from this planet, the energy from the stars, the energy from the universe shows us who we are together.

8-4-98
Total Destruction

Total destruction, eye soars, what a pity, these are the signs of our modern day city. Vacant land, buildings falling down, things seem to get worse before they finally turn around.

Visions of a new beginning, visions for city hall, visions of a city that could be but isn't at all. Twenty years down the road, their vision has come true , but at what cost for people like me and you. They seized our land, bought it for a dime, called it progress, and if you didn't have any money, you were just at the end of the line.

3-25-2000
Total Energy

The body, it gets tired, but with the mind, you can still see that this World we live on is total energy. We created this planet, just you and me, with this incredible force that we call energy. The energy that we give, we also receive by sharing with this planet our so-called reality.

Life is but an illusion, reality is too, but to create this illusion, it's the energy that we use. The energy of this planet will never run down, as long as we exist, it will always be around. The Oceans, the Rivers, the flowers, and the trees are a part of this life force, this thing we call energy.

6-28-98
Traveler

I am but a traveler, a traveler in time that has come across many light-years and through the valleys of the mind. Each one of us has had a mission, each one of us has had a goal to somehow enlighten the planet so the vision could unfold.

We are all God's children, but if the story be told, we are the ones who created this planet and all the gifts it holds. Beliefs make things happen, beliefs make a story come true, beliefs in other people hold the vision inside for you.

By Jim Lozen

5-25-95
Twin Towers

September 11th, the day we all died, if only just a little, we all died inside. The clock was ticking, it was 8:45, the workday was just beginning, no one survived. It brought us together, we all appeared as one, it brought us together under the morning's hot sun.

We dug with our hands, implements too, we dug with anything that we could use. The clock kept ticking as the days passed by, revenge was in our hearts, and only God knew why. Children with pictures looking for Dad, Mothers with stories of the good times they had. Memories are all that they will ever be, memories of the men who gave their lives for liberty.

6-30-96
Twinless Twin

Your twinless twin dies at birth, or there would be two of you. He's your link to the other side to help you make it through. He gives you insights and feelings that other people don't have, and he's always there to help you out when times are bad.

Some people think you're crazy for talking to someone who's not there, but he's like a Guardian Angel, he's everywhere. He's your free pass to Heaven when the time comes, he's got his foot in the gate, and he's just waiting on one.

7-4-2000
Two-Faced

Angels, Devils, we are all the same, Hell is on this planet, and there is no one to blame. Destiny guides us like a falling star, but the energy of this planet shows us just who we really are.

The day starts with the morning dawn, which nurtures this planet so life will go on, then comes the setting sun, and the beast comes out that's within everyone. We have to learn to domesticate this fool before we can share the love upon this planet the way we were supposed to do. Love is the answer, love is the key, love is the destination of our so-called reality.

When our reality changes and our planet has become one, the Universe will call to us, "and it has already begun."

4-23-97
Two

There are two people inside of me, there's the one you see, and then there's the real me. I've been writing now for a couple years, and the one inside is still trying to bust out of here.

I've got to keep him deep down inside, because he couldn't handle the real world, so he would just have to hide. I wonder how many people there are who are just like me, who are scared to set their inner self free.

6-22-2000
The Ultimate You

The universe is infinite, and so are we, we create what we want and desire what we need! Our bodies are dormant, and we will not age, we will not get sick, because God made us that way.

Everything that happens, everything that you do is made by a choice that you made, this will happen to you. Your beliefs and your desires, they will all become true in a world filled with Magic, this is the Ultimate you.

Some people don't know this, most people won't even agree, but the God Force is in everything that you can see. Desire, that's all anyone has to do, just desire, and all of your dreams can and will become true.

11-22-97
Understanding

Earth, wind, fire, and rain, through them, our body is formed and sustained. The art of understanding and enlightenment, they're both the same, there is no wrong or right, there's never anyone to blame.

The knowledge that is with us, it's buried deep within our mind, and it can come through at any given time. You don't need an education, you don't need a college degree, because the knowledge is always with us, it's cosmic energy.

The death of a loved one, the death of a friend isn't really dying, because it's never the end. We will live forever, but our bodies may die, but we will live forever with the energy of the mind.

6-16-97
Wrong or Right

There's is no wrong, there is no right, there is just darkness throughout the night. The future is now, the present is here, it comes together, bringing everything near. You create with your mind as the energy flows, you have everything you need as the energy goes.

Beliefs, untruths, and little lies have created this world we all live inside. The world of enlightenment is just a stone's throw ahead, and it's easy to get to, it's just like falling out of bed.

When you get there, when you arrive, you'll see the world as it should be from the other side. No hatred, no killing everything, as it should be, thanks to that God-given energy.

11-28-98
Valhalla

The Vikings, they called it Valhalla, but it's called Nirvana at this point in time, it's a place you can only enter through the Valleys of the mind. The Masters that have already been there are the Teachers of today, they teach all over this Planet the words that we cannot say.

Teachers of Old, Teachers of New, but NOBODY understands them, and NOBODY has a clue. They're here to remind us of Who and What we are, they're here to remind us that we too can REACH for the STARS, so it doesn't really matter what we say or what we do, because one day when you're TOTALY open, it will all just dawn on you.

7-12-96
Vets

You don't read about the guys who gave their lives in Nam or the paralyzed vets that were once very strong.

America has just shoved them to the rear like so much garbage and hopes they disappear.

We were sent to Nam to fight a war we were never meant to win, and half of us never came home again.

It happened a long time ago, but it seems like yesterday, because some of us just won't let go.

America has made a lot of junkies and alcoholics out of its Vietnam vets, but they just do this to try to forget.

4-18-2000
Vibrations

Energy has color, it's the vibrations of the mind, the vibrations of the body are the auras that you will find. The colors are like a river that changes from night to day, it all depends on the thoughts you think and the words you happen to say.

You are like a "Mood Ring," all the colors known to man, all the colors of the rainbow are brought across this land. When things get tough, the auras start glowing, and you will change to a crimson red or blue, but this energy that you create is impossible to use. Bright red is the life force that's born to every child, but this color changes to a yellow or green after just a little while. Everything has an aura, everything is energy, everything under the sun is just like you and me.

5-12-95
Victim

To be the victim is the crime, because you have to live with what happened all the time.

You keep going through it in your mind and what you could have done at the time.

Now I have a lot of things that I could have tried, but if he had a gun, I could have died.

I teach karate, so I'll just react, but if he had a gun, I could be lying on my back.

The thoughts that go through a victim's mind can get pretty scary, and they could be there for quite a long time.

6-13-96
Vietnamese Lady

I didn't speak her language, and she didn't speak mine, but we had a very special way of entering each other's mind. I knew what she was thinking, and she knew every thought of mine, she was the only woman I'll ever love until the end of time.

She was a Vietnamese lady, and I was just a GI, but we had something between us that we thought would never die, but then something happened, and Vietnam was gone, and so was my Vietnamese lady whom I loved so strong.

7-14-02
Waiting for the Moment

Waiting for the moment, waiting for the time when you can call me yours and I can call you mine. This world is funny, everyone is just waiting for the key, but the key is inside of people just like you and me. Time has no meaning, the future has no end, the past is always present as the energy descends.

Waiting for the moment, waiting for the time when this planet will awaken and find that life is divine. This world was created by people just like you and me, with visions in their minds, they created everything you can see.

3-12-2000
Wanting

Wanting is like tomorrow, because it never comes, it's always in the future for everyone. The past is like the present, because it's always there, you can change it if you desire, but most people don't care.

They think because they've already done that, they can't go back and do that again, but it's all in the mind, it's the game that never ends. The past is the future, the future is the past, tomorrow will never come, and the wanting will always last. Desire is the outcome, and now is the time of each day, set yourself upright and get ready to play the game, because we always play that way.

9-22-02
We Are the One

We are going to change this world, just you and me, we are going to change this world with our creative energies. This world is just an illusion that we create with our minds, we create every day, we create all of the time. We create every minute of every single day, we create every hour, no matter what we think do or say.

The energy keeps flowing, for it is just a dream and this world is just an illusion, but it's as real as it seems. Domestication from childhood have brought us to where we are, old dreams and beliefs have made us who we are, it's time to change this world and make it our own, it's time to change this illusion and come back home. Home is where the heart is, and love is who you are, we are the makings of this planet the universe and stars.

11-5-2000
Weird but True

Negative energy is what kills you, and even your fears come into play. You create whatever happens, you even created today. Age is a factor, but age doesn't exist, age is a belief that you created, which brought about all of this.

Wrong or right, right or wrong makes no difference, because neither belong. True or false, that's all you need, because true or false will never affect you or me. This world's funny in that way, because you have to watch what you think or say. You create everything throughout time, you even created this little rhyme.

8-22-04
What If

The mind is a weapon, energy is the key to unlocking the Universe, which is an illusion and also our reality. We've created the passion, the hate, and the love with this little thing called energy, which this planet is made of. You've created your brother, your sister too, you've created everything and anything that is a part of you.

We've created the month, the time, and the year, when in reality, it is now, and this will never disappear. Age, death, it is the reality of the past, for this is our future, where we will always last.

1-8-97
What Is Love?

Love is what you make of it, it's born deep within your heart. Love has always been there, it's been there from the start. You might have problems, all of us do, but when you have love in your heart, the light just seems to shine right on through. Love is the kindness that you show to your brothers every day, love is that special thing that you do in your own very special way.

10-18-03
While There's Still Time

You're the energy within, you're the energy that is me, you're the energy of this universe, you're everything that I see. We live in the future, but we think in the past, and everything that we do will always last. We are the energy of the universe, you and me, the energy of this place that we call reality.

Time doesn't exist, it only survives by the beliefs that we have that have formed inside. Look at the children, free as can be, because they haven't adopted our realities. The choice is yours, it's not mine, do unto others while there's still time.

3-17-01
White Pure Light

The desire to want you, the desire to need, the desire to hold you, I have all of these. The dreams that come to me all through the night are choices that I can make with the morning's light. They're just coded messages, little clues sent by this energy, this energy that I use.

A radiant beam of white pure light that shines in the heavens both day and night. This energy that I speak of, this energy that I use, this energy resides in both me and you. There for the taking, there for the need, there for the desire, this energy belongs to you and me.

We are all "GODS," each and every one, we have created this planet and everything under the Sun. If you still haven't figured this out yet, if you still haven't got a clue, our bodies are dormant, but the choice is yours, and it's still up to you.

1-22-97
Woman

I've got this woman by my side, but she's just there, she's along for the ride. She doesn't do anything that I can't do, she's a wolf in sheep's clothing, and that's something that I can't use.

I fell in "LOVE" back in '92, but that's before she moved in, and now she's always out on the run. She started messing around with other guys and doing drugs just to get high. She's the type of woman no one really needs, but she's the type of woman everyone wants to see.

Working

It doesn't really matter to me, and I guess it never did, as long as I've got a job, and I'm living the life that I live.

Now I'm getting older each and every day, and it's getting kind of late in life to try and change my ways.

Some people think I'm crazy for doing the things that I do, but they can't realize the benefits unless they do , the things that I do.

7-12-96
Worldview

The Worldview will change within the next couple years, and the World we know will seem to disappear. A great catastrophe will come wreaking havoc on everyone.

The continents will move like they did a long time ago, creating new and different climates wherever you go.

The Earth will shake and tremble, spitting fire from below, and great rivers of lava will begin to flow. Money won't mean what it did once before, and the fight for survival will begin once more.

7-13-95
World Peace

World peace is something that has to start with you, it's not something you're born with, but it's something you have got to do.

Peace is different for everyone, mine comes from teaching karate and through meditation, and that's not for everyone.

When I'm at my level, my mind really soars, I have this feeling of complete freedom I never had before, and when I'm teaching karate to my kids, you have the greatest sense of accomplishment to see that they can do what you just did.

So if everyone will take some advice from me, you'll find your own little niche in life, and it will set you free.

5-16-04
Your Mind Is a Weapon

Your mind is a weapon, and your brain is the key, but this doesn't mean a thing if you can't believe. The choices are yours, there's no wrong or right, and these choices you make will guide you into the light.

You can't die here, I don't know if you'll understand, but we are all a part of the energy, this energy of the land. We created this planet, you and me, we created and will reside here for all eternity. This isn't the beginning, and this isn't the end, we've been here before, and we'll be here again. We've created this planet, we've created these rules, there's nothing in this world that we can't do.

12-31-03
Year's End

The old year is ending tonight at twelve, and the new year is beginning at that time as well. Santa is gone for another year, memories are fading and soon will disappear. The rebirth of this planet, the rebirth of time starts in one, one's own mind. You create your needs, wants, and desires too, you create everything and anything that you can use.

The energy of this planet, it's just a tool, a tool to be used by everyone, even me and you.

You and Me

Let's fly to the mountains or down to the sea, let's drive down the highway, baby, just you and me. Let's look at the stars or the moon up above, let's talk about things that we both love.

You're the only girl who's ever meant something to me. Let's spend the night together, baby, just you and me. We'll go down to breakfast at about half past eight, then we'll fly to the mountains or down to the sea, we'll watch the sun come up, baby, just you and me.